KATIA

LEO TOLSTOY

TRUE SIGN
PUBLISHING HOUSE

Published by True Sign Publishing House
Address: SY. No. 21/2 & 21/3, Sonnenahalli,
Krishnarajapural, Bengaluru,
Karnataka - 560049 India
E-mail: truesignbooks@gmail.com
Website: www.truesign.in

Katia
Author: Leo Tolstoy

ISBN: 978-93-5462-922-8

First Edition: 2022

Contents

CHAPTER-I

WE were in mourning for our mother, who had died the preceding autumn, and we had spent all the winter alone in the country—Macha, Sonia and I.

Macha was an old family friend, who had been our governess and had brought us all up, and my memories of her, like my love for her, went as far back as my memories of myself.

Sonia was my younger sister.

The winter had dragged by, sad and sombre, in our old country-house of Pokrovski. The weather had been cold, and so windy that the snow was often piled high above our windows; the panes were almost always cloudy with a coating of ice; and throughout the whole season we were shut in, rarely finding it possible to go out of the house.

It was very seldom that any one came to see us, and our few visitors brought neither joy nor cheerfulness to our house. They all had mournful faces, spoke low, as if they were afraid of waking some one, were careful not to laugh, sighed and often shed tears when they looked at me, and above all at the sight of my poor Sonia in her little black frock. Everything in the house still savored of death; the affliction, the horror of the last agony yet reigned in the air. Mamma's chamber was shut up, and I felt a painful dread and yet an irresistible longing to peep furtively into the chill, desolate place as I passed it every night on my way to bed.

I was at this time seventeen years old, and the very year of her death Mamma had intended to remove to the city, in order to introduce me into society. The loss of my mother had been a great sorrow to me; but I must confess that to this grief had been added another, that of seeing myself—young, beautiful as I heard from every one that I was,—condemned to vegetate during a second winter in the country, in a barren solitude. Even before the end of this winter, the feeling of regret, of isolation, and, to speak plainly, of ennui, had so gained upon me that I scarcely ever left my own room, never opened my piano, and never even took a book in my hand. If Macha urged me to occupy myself with something I would reply: "I do not wish to, I cannot," and far down in my soul a voice kept asking: "What is the use? Why 'do something'—no matter what—when the best of my life is wearing away so in pure loss? Why?" And to this "Why?" I had no answer except tears.

I was told that I was growing thin and losing my beauty, but this gave me not the slightest concern. Why, and for whom, should I take interest in it? It seemed to me that my entire life was to drift slowly away in this desert, borne down by this hopeless suffering, from which, given up to my own resources alone, I had no longer the strength, nor even the wish, to set myself free.

Towards the end of the winter Macha became seriously uneasy about me, and determined come what might to take me abroad. But for this, money was essential, and as yet we knew little of our resources beyond the fact that we were to succeed to our mother's inheritance; however, we were in daily expectation of a visit from our guardian, who was to examine the condition of our affairs.

He came at last, late in March.

"Thank Heaven!" said Macha to me one day, when I was wandering like a shadow from one corner to another, perfectly idle, without a thought in my head or a wish in my heart: "Sergius Mikaïlovitch has sent word that he will be here before dinner.—You must rouse yourself, my little Katia," she added; "what will he think of you? He loves you both so much!"

Sergius Mikaïlovitch was our nearest neighbor, and though much his junior had been the friend of our dead father. Besides the pleasant change which his arrival might cause in our life, by making it possible for us to leave the country, I had been too much accustomed, from my childhood, to love and respect him, for Macha not to divine while urging me to rouse myself, that still another change might be worked and that, of all my acquaintances, he was the one before whom I would be most unwilling to appear in an unfavorable light. Not only did I feel the old attachment for Sergius Mikaïlovitch which was shared by every one in the house, from Sonia, who was his god-daughter, down to the under-coachman, but this attachment had derived a peculiar character from a few words Mamma had once let fall before me. She had said that he was just the husband that she would have wished for me. At the moment such an idea had appeared to me very extraordinary and even somewhat disagreeable; the hero of my imagination was totally different. My own hero was to be slender, delicate, pale, and melancholy. Sergius Mikaïlovitch, on the contrary, was no longer young, he was tall and large, full of vigor, and, so far as I could judge, had an extremely pleasant temper; nevertheless my mother's remark had made a strong impression on my imagination. This had happened six years before, when I was only eleven, when he still said "*thou*" to me, played with me, and gave me the name of *La petite violette*, yet ever since that day I had always felt some secret misgivings whenever I had asked myself the question what I should do if he should suddenly take a fancy to marry me?

A little before dinner, to which Macha had added a dish of spinach and a sweet *entre mets* Sergius Mikaïlovitch arrived. I was looking out of the window when his light sledge approached, and as he turned the corner of the house I hastily drew back into the drawing-room, not wishing to let him see that I had been watching for him the least in the world. But upon hearing sounds in the ante-chamber, his strong voice, and Macha's footsteps, I lost patience and went myself to meet him. He was holding Macha's hand, and talking to her in a raised voice, smiling. When he perceived me, he stopped and looked at me for some moments without saluting me; it embarrassed me a good deal, and I felt myself blush.

"Ah! is it possible that this is you, Katia?" he said in his frank, decided tone, disengaging his hand and approaching me.

"Can people change so! How you have grown! Yesterday a violet! To-day the full rose!"

His large hand clasped mine, pressing it so cordially, so strongly, that he almost hurt me. I had thought he might kiss me, and bent a little towards him; but he only caught it a second time, and looked me straight in the eyes with his bright, steady glance.

I had not seen him for six years. He was much changed, older, browner, and his whiskers, which he had allowed to grow, were not particularly becoming to him; but he had the same simple manners, the same open, honest face, with its marked features, eyes sparkling with intelligence, and smile as sweet as a child's.

At the end of five minutes he was no longer on the footing of a mere visitor, but on that of an intimate guest with us all, and even the servants manifested their joy at his arrival, by the eager zeal with which they served him.

He did not act at all like a neighbor who, coming to a house for the first time after the mother's death, thinks it necessary to bring with him a solemn countenance; on the contrary, he was gay, talkative, and did not say a single word about Mamma, so that I began to think this indifference on the part of a man standing in such near relation to us very strange, and rather unseemly. But I soon saw that it was far from being indifference, and read in his intention a considerateness for which I could not help being grateful.

In the evening Macha gave us tea in the drawing-room where it had been usually served during Mamma's lifetime. Sonia and I sat near her; Gregory found one of Papa's old pipes, and brought it to our guardian, who began to pace up and down the room according to his old fashion.

"What terrible changes in this house, when one thinks of it!" said he, stopping suddenly.

"Yes," replied Macha with a sigh; and replacing the top of the samovar, she looked up at Sergius Mikaïlovitch, almost ready to burst into tears.

"No doubt you remember your father?" he asked me.

"A little."

"How fortunate it would be for you, now, to have him still!" he observed slowly, with a thoughtful air, casting a vague glance into vacancy over my head. And he added more slowly still:

"I loved your father very much...."

I thought I detected a new brightness in his eyes at this moment.

"And now God has taken away our mother also!" exclaimed Macha. Dropping her napkin on the tea-tray, she pulled out her handkerchief and began to cry.

"Yes, there have been terrible changes in this house!"

He turned away as he spoke.

Then, a moment after: "Katia Alexandrovna," he said, in a louder voice, "play me something!"

I liked the tone of frank, friendly authority with which he made this request; I rose and went to him.

"Here, play me this," said he, opening my Beethoven at the adagio of the sonata, *Quasi una fantasia*. "Let us see how you play," he continued, taking his cup of tea to drink in a corner of the room.

I know not why, but I felt it would be impossible either to refuse or to put forward a plea of playing badly; on the contrary, I submissively sat down at the piano and began to play as well as I could, although I was afraid of his criticism, knowing his excellent taste in music.

In the tone of this *adagio* there was a prevalent sentiment which by association carried me away to the conversation before tea, and, guided by this impression, I played tolerably well, it seemed. But he would not let me play the *scherzo*.

"No, you will not play it well," said he, coming to me, "stop with that first movement,—which has not been bad! I see that you comprehend music."

This praise, certainly moderate enough, delighted me so that I felt my color rise. It was something so new and agreeable to me to have the friend, the *equal* of my father, speak to me alone, seriously, and no longer as though he were talking to a child as he used to do.

He talked to me about my father, telling me how they suited each other, and what a pleasant life they had led together while I was occupied solely with my playthings and school-books; and what he said revealed my father to me in a light quite new to me, for the first time I seemed to know fully his simple goodness. My guardian questioned me as to what I liked, what I read, what I intended doing, and gave me advice. I had no longer beside me the gay talker, delighting in badinage, but a man serious, frank, friendly, for whom I felt involuntary respect, while at the same time I was conscious of being in perfect sympathy with him. This consciousness was pleasing to me, nevertheless there was a certain tension in conversing with him. Every word I uttered left me timid; I wished so much to deserve in my own person the affection which at present I only received because I was my father's daughter!

After putting Sonia to bed, Macha rejoined us, and began to pour out to Sergius Mikaïlovitch her lamentations on the score of my apathy, which resulted she complained in my rarely having a single word to say.

"Then she has not told me the most important thing of all," he answered, smiling, and shaking his head at me with an air of reproach.

"What had I to tell?" I replied: "that I was bored?—but that will pass away." (And indeed it now seemed to me, not only that my ennui would pass away, but that it was something already gone by, which could not return.)

"It is not well not to know how to bear solitude:—is it possible that you are truly a 'grown young lady'?"

"I believe so!" I answered smiling.

"No, no, or at least a naughty young lady, who only lives to be admired, and who, when she finds herself isolated, gives way, and no longer enjoys anything; all for show, nothing for herself."

"You have a lovely idea of me, it seems!" I answered, to say something.

"No," he returned, after a moment's silence; "it is not in vain that you have that resemblance to your father; *there is something in you*!"

Again those kind, steadfast eyes exerted their charm over me, filling me with strange emotion.

I noticed for the first time at this moment that the face which to a casual glance seemed so gay, the expression, so peculiarly his own, where at first one seemed to read only serenity, afterwards revealed more and more clearly, a reserve of deep thought and a shade of sadness.

"You should not feel ennui," he said, "you have music, which you are able to understand, books, study; you have before you a whole life, for which the present is the only moment to prepare yourself, so that hereafter you may not have to repine. In a year it will be too late."

He spoke to me like a father or an uncle, and I understood that he was making an effort to come to my level. I was a little offended that he should think me so much below him, and on the other hand, it was gratifying to feel that he cared to make the effort for my sake.

The rest of the evening was devoted to a business conversation between him and Macha.

"And now, good-night, my dear Katia," said he, rising, approaching me, and taking my hand.

"When shall we see each other again?" asked Macha.

"In the spring," he replied, still holding my hand; "I am now going to Danilovka" (our other estate); "I must look into matters there and make some necessary arrangements, then I have to go to Moscow upon business of my own, and later—or in the summer—we shall see each other again."

"Why do you go for so long a time?" I asked, dejectedly; for I was already hoping to see him every day, and it was with a sudden sinking of my heart that I thought of again battling with my ennui. Probably my eyes and voice let this be guessed.

"Come, occupy yourself more; drive away the blues!" he said in a voice that seemed to me too placid and cold. "In the spring I will hold an examination," he added, dropping my hand without looking at me.

We accompanied him to the ante-chamber, where he hurriedly put on his pelisse, and again his eyes seemed to avoid mine.

"He is taking very useless trouble!" I said to myself, "can it be possible that he thinks he is giving me too great a pleasure by looking at me!—An excellent man—Perfectly good.... But that is all."

We remained awake a long time that night talking, not of him, but of the employment of the ensuing summer, of where and how we should spend the winter. Mighty question, yet why? To me it appeared perfectly simple and evident that life was to consist in being happy, and in the future I could imagine nothing but happiness, so suddenly had our sombre old dwelling at Pokrovski filled itself with life and light.

CHAPTER-II

THE spring came. My former ennui had disappeared, and in exchange I felt the dreamy vernal sadness, woven of unknown hopes and unslaked desires. But my life was no longer the existence I had led during the early winter; I occupied myself with Sonia, with music, with studies, and I often went into the garden, to spend a long, long, time in wandering alone through the shady walks, or in sitting motionless upon some quiet bench. God knows what I was thinking, what I was wishing, what I was hoping! Sometimes for whole nights, especially if it was moonlight, I would remain kneeling at my window with my elbows on the sill; morning would find me there; and sometimes, without Macha's knowing it, I would steal down into the garden again after I was in my simple night-dress, and fly through the dew to the little pond; once I even went out into the fields, and spent the rest of the night roaming alone about the park.

Now it is difficult for me to recall, still less to comprehend, the reveries which at this period filled my imagination. If I can succeed in remembering them, I can hardly believe that these reveries were my own, so strange were they, so outside of real life.

At the end of May, Sergius Mikaïlovitch, as he had promised, returned from his journey.

The first time he came to see us was in the evening, when we were not expecting him at all. We were sitting on the terrace, preparing to take tea. The garden was in full verdure, and at Pokrovski nightingales had their homes on all sides in the thick shrubbery. Here and there, large clumps of lilacs raised their heads, enamelled with the white or pale purple of their opening flowers. The leaves in the birch alleys seemed transparent in the rays of the setting sun. The terrace lay in refreshing shade, and the light evening dew was gathering upon the grass. In the court-yard behind the garden were heard the sounds of closing day, and the lowing of cows returning to their stable; poor half-witted Nikone came along the path at the foot of the terrace with his huge watering-pot, and soon the torrents of cool water traced in darkening circles over the newly-dug earth of the dahlia beds. Beside us on the terrace, the shining samovar hissed and sputtered on the white cloth, flanked by cream, pancakes, and sweetmeats. Macha, with her plump hands, was dipping the cups in hot water like a good housekeeper. As to me, with an appetite sharpened by my late bath, I could not wait for tea, but was eating a crust of bread soaked in fresh, rich cream. I had on a linen blouse with loose sleeves, and my damp hair was bound in a handkerchief.

Macha was the first to perceive him.

"Ah! Sergius Mikaïlovitch!" she cried; "we were just talking about you."

I rose to run in and change my dress; but he met me as I reached the door.

"Come, Katia, no ceremony in the country," said he, smiling, and looking at my head and my handkerchief, "you have no scruples before Gregory,—I can be Gregory to you."

But at the same time it darted into my mind that he was not looking at me precisely as Gregory would have done, and this embarrassed me.

"I will be back directly," I replied, drawing away from him.

"What is wrong about it?" he exclaimed, following me, "one might take you for a little peasant girl!"

"How strangely he looked at me," I thought, as I hastened up-stairs to dress myself. "At last, thank Heaven, here he is, and we shall be gayer!" And with a parting glance at the mirror I flew down again, not even trying to conceal my eager delight, and reached the terrace, out of breath. He was sitting near the table, talking to Macha about our business matters. Noticing me, he gave me a smile, and went on talking. Our affairs, he said, were in very satisfactory condition. We had nothing to do but to finish our country summer, and then we could go, either to St. Petersburg for Sonia's education, or abroad.

"That would be very well, if you would come abroad with us," said Macha, "but by ourselves we should be like people lost in the woods."

"Ah! would to Heaven I could go around the world with you," was the half-jesting, half-serious answer.

"Well and good," said I, "let us go around the world then!"

He smiled and shook his head.

"And my mother? And my business? Come, we will let the tour of the world alone, now, and you can tell me how you have passed your time. Can it be possible that you have had the blues again?"

When I told him that I had been able, without him, to employ myself and not to yield to ennui, and Macha had confirmed the good account, he praised me, with the same words and looks of encouragement he would have used to a child, and as if he had a perfect right to do so. It seemed to me quite natural that I should tell him frankly and minutely everything I had done that was right, and also, on the contrary, own to him, as if in the confessional, whatever I had done that might deserve his censure. The evening was so beautiful that, when the tea-tray was carried away, we remained upon the terrace, and I found the conversation so interesting that I only gradually became aware that all the sounds from the house were ceasing around us. Upon all sides arose the penetrating night perfume of flowers, the turf was drenched with heavy dew, the nightingale in a lilac bush near us was executing his roulades, stopping abruptly at the sound of our voices. The starry sky seemed to stoop close above our heads.

What warned me that night had come, was the swift, heavy rush of a bat beneath the awning of the terrace, and its blind, terrified circling around my white dress. I fell back against the wall, and almost cried out, but with another dull swoop it was off again and lost in the blackness of the garden.

"How I love your Pokrovski," said Sergius Mikaïlovitch, interrupting the conversation.... "One could linger for a lifetime on this terrace!"

"Well," said Macha, "linger!"

"Ah, yes! linger; but life—does not pause!"

"Why do you not marry?" continued Macha; "you would make an excellent husband!"

"Why?" he repeated, smiling. "People long ago, ceased to count me a marriageable man!"

"What!" replied Macha, "thirty-six years old, and already you pretend to be tired of living?"

"Yes, certainly, and even so tired that I desire nothing but rest. To marry, one must have something else to offer. There, ask Katia," he added, pointing me out with a nod "Girls of her age are the ones for marriage. For us ... our rôle is to enjoy their happiness."

There was a secret melancholy, a certain tension in the tone of his voice, which did not escape me. He kept silence a moment; neither Macha nor I said anything.

"Imagine now," he resumed, turning towards the table again, "if all at once, by some deplorable accident, I should marry a young girl of seventeen, like Katia Alexandrovna! That is a very good example, and I am pleased that it applies so well to the point ... there could not be a better instance."

I began to laugh, but I could not at all understand what pleased him so much, nor to what it applied so well.

"Come, now, tell me the truth, 'hand on heart,'" he went on, turning to me with a bantering air, "would it not be a great misfortune for you, to bind your life to a man already old, who has had his day, and wants nothing except to stay just where he is, while you,—Heaven knows where you would not want to run off to, as the fancy took you!"

I felt uncomfortable, and was silent, not knowing very well what to say in reply.

"I am not making a proposal for your hand," said he, laughing, "but, now, tell us the truth are you dreaming of such a husband, as you wander through your alleys in the evening, and would he not be a great misfortune?"

"Not so great a misfortune ..." I began.

"And not so great a boon, either," he finished for me.

"Yes ... but I may be mistaken...."

He interrupted me again.

"You see?... she is perfectly right.... I like her honesty, and am delighted that we have had this conversation. I will add that—to me—it would have been a supreme misfortune!"

"What an original you are! you have not changed in the least!" said Macha, leaving the terrace to order supper to be served.

After her departure we were silent, and all was still around us. Then the solitary nightingale recommenced, not his abrupt, undecided notes of early evening, but his night song, slow and tranquil, whose thrilling cadence filled the garden; and from far down the ravine came for the first time a response from another nightingale. The one near us was mute for a moment, listening, then burst out anew in a rapture of song, louder and clearer than before. Their voices resounded, calm and supreme, amid that world of night which is their own and which we inhabit as aliens. The gardener went by, on his way to his bed in the orange-house, we heard his heavy boots on the path as he went farther and farther from us. Some one in the direction of the mountain blew two shrill, quick notes on a whistle, then all was still once more. Scarcely a leaf was heard to move; yet all at once the awning of the terrace puffed out slowly, stirred by a breath of air, and a more penetrating perfume stole up to us from below. The silence embarrassed me, but I did not know what to say. I looked at him. His eyes, bright in the darkness, were fixed upon me.

"It is good to live in this world!" he murmured.

I know not why, but at the words I sighed.

"Well?" he questioned.

"Yes, it is good to live in this world!" I repeated.

Again the silence fell upon us, and again I felt ill at ease. I could not get it out of my head that I had hurt him, by agreeing with him that he was old; I would have liked to console him, but did not know how to set about it.

"But good-bye!" he said, rising, "my mother expects me to supper. I have hardly seen her to-day."

"I would have liked to play you my new sonata."

"Another time," he replied coldly, at least so it seemed to me; then, moving off a step, he said with a careless gesture: "Good-bye!"

I was more than ever convinced that I had given him pain, and this distressed me. Macha and I went with him, as far as the porch, and stood there awhile looking down the road where he had disappeared. When we no longer caught the slightest echo from his horse's feet, I began to walk about the terrace and watch the garden, and I remained a long time there, amid the heavy mist that deadened all the sounds of night, busy seeing and hearing whatever my fancy chose to make me see and hear.

He came a second time, a third time, and the little embarrassment caused by our strange conversation soon vanished, and never returned.

Throughout the whole summer he came to see us two or three times a week; I was so accustomed to him that, when a longer time than usual passed without his coming, it seemed to me painful to live alone; I was secretly indignant with him, and thought he was behaving badly in thus deserting me. He transformed himself for me, as it were, into a friendly comrade; inducing the most sincere frankness on my part, giving me advice and encouragement, scolding me sometimes, checking me when necessary. But despite these efforts to remain always upon my level, I was conscious that, besides all I knew of him, there existed within him an entire world, to which I was a stranger, and he did not think it was necessary to admit me; and this, more than anything else, tended to keep up my feeling of deference, and at the same time to attract me towards him. I knew from Macha and the neighbors that, besides his attentive care of his old mother, with whom he lived, besides his agricultural interests, and our guardianship, he had also on hand certain matters affecting all the nobles, which caused him much trouble and annoyance; but how he faced this complex situation, what were his thoughts, his plans, his hopes, I could never discover from him. If I endeavored to lead the conversation to his own affairs, a certain line appeared upon his brow, which seemed to say: "Stop there, if you please; what is that to you?" And he would immediately speak of something else. At first this offended me, then I grew so accustomed to it that we never talked of anything but what concerned me; which I finally came to think quite a matter of course.

At first, too, I felt some displeasure, (while afterwards, on the contrary, it had a kind of charm,) in seeing the perfect indifference, I might almost say contempt, which he showed for my appearance. Never, by word or look, did he give the least idea that he thought me pretty; far from it, he frowned and began to laugh if any one remarked before him that I was "not bad-looking." He even took pleasure in criticizing the defects in my face, and teasing me about them. The fashionable dresses, the coiffures, with which Macha delighted to adorn me on our holidays, only excited his raillery, which chagrined my good Macha not a little, and at first disconcerted me. Macha, who had settled in her own mind that I was pleasing to Sergius Mikaïlovitch, could not at all comprehend why he did not prefer that a woman whom he admired should appear at her best. But I soon discovered what was the matter. He wished to believe that I was not coquettish. As soon as I understood this there no longer remained a trace of coquetry in my dress, hair, or manner; it was replaced—usual and shallow little trick—by another coquetry, the assumption of simplicity, before I had attained the point of really being artless. I saw that he loved me: whether as a child or woman I had not hitherto asked myself: this love was dear to me, and feeling that he considered me the best girl in the world, I could not help wishing that the delusion might continue to blind him. And indeed I deceived him almost involuntarily. But in deluding him, I was nevertheless growing more what he thought me. I felt that it would be better and more worthy of him to unveil to him the good points of my soul rather than those of my person. My hair, my hands, my face, my carriage, whatever they might be, whether good or bad,—it seemed to me he could appreciate at one glance, and that he knew very well that, had I desired to deceive him, I could add nothing at all to my exterior. My soul, on the contrary, he did not know: because he loved it, because just at this time it was in full process of growth and development, and finally because in such a matter it was easy to deceive him, and that I was in fact deceiving him. What relief I felt in his presence, when once I comprehended all this! The causeless agitation, the need of movement, which in some way oppressed me, completely disappeared. It seemed to me henceforth that whether opposite or beside me, whether standing or sitting, whether I wore my hair dressed high or low, he looked at me always with satisfaction, that he now knew me entirely; and I imagined that he was as well pleased with me, as I myself was. I verily believe that if, contrary to his custom, he had suddenly said to me as others did that I was pretty, I should even have been a little sorry. But, on the other hand, what joy, what serenity, I felt in the depth of my soul, if, upon the occasion of my expressing some thought or letting fall a few words, he looked at me attentively and said in a moved tone which he strove to render light and jesting:

"Yes, yes, there is *something* in you! You are a good girl, and I ought to tell you so."

And for what did I receive this recompense which filled my heart with joy and pride? Perhaps because I had said that I sympathized with old Gregory's love for his little daughter, perhaps because I had been affected to tears while reading a poem or a romance, perhaps for preferring Mozart to Schuloff! I was amazed by this new intuition, which enabled me to divine what was good and what one ought to like, though as yet I had no positive knowledge of either. Most of my past habits and tastes were displeasing to him, and a look or an imperceptible movement of his eyebrows was enough to make me understand his disapproval of what I was about to do; while a certain air of slightly disdainful pity, which was peculiar to him, would at once make me believe that I no longer liked what had formerly pleased me. If the thought of giving me advice upon any subject, occurred to him, I knew beforehand what he was going to say to me. He questioned me with a glance, and already this glance had drawn from me the thought he wished to ascertain. All my thoughts, all my feelings during that time, were not my own; they were his, which suddenly became mine, penetrating and illuminating my life. In a manner insensible to me, I began to see everything with other eyes, Macha, my servants, Sonia, as well as myself and my own occupations. The books which formerly I had read only in order to ward off ennui appeared to me all at once one of the greatest charms of life, and for no reason except that we talked, he and I, of books, that we read them together, that he brought them to me. Hitherto I had considered my work with Sonia, the lessons I gave her, as a painful obligation, only fulfilled from a sense of duty; now that he sometimes came to assist at these lessons one of my delights was to observe Sonia's progress. To learn an entire piece of music had always seemed impossible, and now, knowing that he would listen and perhaps applaud it, I thought nothing of going over the same passage forty times in succession, poor Macha would end by stopping her ears with cotton wool, while I would not consider the performance at all tiresome. The old sonatas spoke out under my fingers in a very different and very superior voice. Even Macha, whom I had always known and loved as myself, seemed totally changed. It was only now that I understood that nothing had compelled her to be what she had been to us, a mother, a friend, a slave to our whims and fancies. I comprehended all the abnegation, all the devotion, of this loving creature, I realized the greatness of my obligations to her, and loved her so much the more. He had already taught me to regard our people, our peasants, our drorovиés,[A] our men and women servants, in a totally different light. It is an odd fact, but at seventeen years of age, I was living in the midst of them a far greater stranger to them than to people I had never seen; not once had it crossed my mind that they were beings capable like myself of love, desires, regrets. Our garden, our woods, our fields, which I had known ever since I was born, suddenly became quite new to me, and I began to admire their loveliness. There was no error in the remark which he so often made, that, in life, there was but one certain happiness: to live for others. This had appeared strange

[A] Peasants attached to the household, and not to the soil.

to me, and I had not been able to understand it; but the conviction, unknown even to my own mind, was penetrating little by little into the depths of my heart. In short, he had opened before me a new life, full of present delights, without having in any wise changed or added to my old existence, save by developing each of my own sensations. From my infancy everything around me had remained buried in a sort of silence, only awaiting his presence to lift up a voice, speak to my soul, and fill it with happiness.

Often, in the course of this summer, I would go up to my chamber, throw myself upon my bed, and there, in place of the old anguish of the spring, full of desires and hopes for the future, I would feel myself wrapped in another emotion, that of present happiness. I could not sleep, I would get up and go and sit on the side of Macha's bed, and tell her that I was perfectly happy,—which, as I look back upon it to-day was perfectly needless; she could see it well enough for herself. She would reply that neither had she anything more to wish for, that she too was very happy, and would embrace me. I believed her, so entirely natural and necessary did it seem to me for every one to be happy. But Macha had her night's rest to think of, so, pretending to be angry, she would drive me away from her bed, and drop off to sleep; I, on the contrary, would lie for a long time running over all my reasons for being gladsome. Sometimes I would rise, and begin my prayers a second time, praying in the fulness of my heart that I might thank God better for all the happiness He had granted me. In my chamber all was peaceful; there was no sound save the long-drawn regular breathing of the sleeping Macha, and the ticking of the watch by her side; I would return to bed, murmur a few words, cross myself, or kiss the little cross hanging at my neck. The doors were locked, the shutters fast over the windows, the buzzing of a fly struggling in a corner came to my ear. I could have wished never to leave this room; desired that morning might never come to dissipate the atmosphere impregnated with my soul, that enveloped me. It seemed to me that my dreams, my thoughts, my prayers, were so many animated essences which in this darkness lived with me, fluttered about my pillow, hovered above my head. And every thought was his thought, every feeling his feeling. I did not yet know what love was, I thought that it might always be thus—that it might give itself and ask nothing in return.

CHAPTER-III

ONE day, during the grain harvest, Macha, Sonia, and I, went into the garden after dinner, to our favorite bench under the shade of the linden-trees at the head of the ravine, whence we could see the fields and the woods. For three days Sergius Mikaïlovitch had not been to see us, and we looked for him all the more confidently to-day, as he had promised our intendant to visit the harvest fields.

About two o'clock we saw him coming over the rising ground in the middle of a rye field. Macha, giving me a smile, ordered a servant to bring out some peaches and cherries, which he was very fond of, then stretched herself upon the bench and was soon fast asleep. I broke off a little linden bough, its leaves and bark fresh with young sap, and, while I fanned Macha, went on with my reading, not without turning every instant to watch the field-path by which he must come to us. Sonia had established herself on a linden root, and was busy putting up a green arbor for her dolls.

The day was very warm, without wind, it seemed as if we were in a hot-house; the clouds, lying in a low circle upon the horizon, had looked angry in the morning, and there had been a threat of storm, which, as was always the case, had excited and agitated me. But since mid-day the clouds had dispersed, the sun was free in a clear sky, the thunder was only muttering at a single point, rolling slowly through the depths of a heavy cloud which, seeming to unite earth and heaven, blended with the dust of the fields, and was furrowed by pale zig-zags of distant lightning. It was evident that for us at least there was no more to be dreaded for that day. In the part of the road running behind the garden there was continual sound and motion, now the slow, long grind of a wagon loaded with sheaves, now the quick jolt of the empty telégas[B] as they passed each other, or the rapid steps of the drivers, whose white

[B] Russian cart, consisting of a flat frame-work of bark, between four wheels.

smocks we could see fluttering as they hurried along. The thick dust neither blew away nor fell, it remained suspended above the hedges, a hazy background for the clear green leaves of the garden trees. Farther off, about the barn, resounded more voices, more grinding wheels; and I could see the yellow sheaves, brought in the carts to the enclosure, being tossed off into the air, and heaped up, until at length I could distinguish the stacks, rising like oval sharp-roofed buildings, and the silhouettes of the peasants swarming about them. Presently, there were new *telégas* moving in the dusty fields, new piles of yellow sheaves, and in the distance the wheels, the voices, the chanted songs.

The dust and heat invaded everything, except our little favorite nook of the garden. Yet on all sides, in the dust and heat, the blaze of the burning sun, the throng of laborers chattered, made merry, and kept in continual movement. As for me, I looked at Macha, sleeping so sweetly on our bench, her face shaded by her cambric handkerchief; the black juicy cherries on the plate; our light, dazzlingly clean dresses, the carafe of clear water, where the sun's rays were playing in a little rainbow; and I felt a sense of rare comfort. "What must I do?" thought I; "perhaps it is wicked to be so happy? But can we diffuse our happiness around us? How, and to whom, can we wholly consecrate ourselves—ourselves and this very happiness?"

The sun had disappeared behind the tops of the old birch-trees bordering the path, the dust had subsided; the distances of the landscape stood out, clear and luminous, under the slanting rays; the clouds had dispersed entirely, long ago; on the other side of the trees I could see, near the barn, the pointed tops rise upon three new stacks of grain, and the peasants descend from them; finally, for the last time that day, the *telégas* passed rapidly, making the air resound with their noisy jolts; the women were going homewards, singing, their rakes on their shoulders, and their binding withes hanging at their girdles; and still Sergius Mikaïlovitch did not come, although long ago I had seen him at the foot of the mountain. Suddenly he appeared at the end of the path, from a direction where I had not been looking for him at all, for he had to skirt the ravine to reach it. Raising his hat he came towards me, his face lighted up with sudden joy. At the sight of Macha, still asleep, his eyes twinkled, he bit his lip, and began tip-toeing elaborately. I saw at once that he was in one of those fits of causeless gayety which I liked so much in him, and which, between ourselves, we called "*le transport sauvage*." At such times he was like a boy just let out of school, his whole self from head to foot instinct with delight and happiness.

"How do you do, little violet, how goes the day with you? Well?" said he, in a low voice, coming near and pressing my hand.... "And with me? oh, charmingly, also!" he replied to my similar question, "to-day I am really not over thirteen years old; I would like to ride a stick-horse,—I want to climb the trees!"

"*Le transport sauvage!*" I commented, looking into his laughing eyes, and feeling this *transport sauvage* take possession of me also.

"Yes," he murmured, at the same time raising his eyebrows with an enquiring glance, and keeping back a smile. "But why are you so furious with our poor Macha Karlovna?"

In fact I then became conscious that, while I was gazing up at him and continuing to brandish my linden bough, I had whipped off Macha's handkerchief, and was sweeping her face with the leaves. I could not help laughing.

"And she will say she has not been asleep," I said, whispering, as if afraid of waking her; but I did not do it altogether for that,—it was so delightful to whisper when I spoke to him!

He moved his lips in almost dumb show, imitating me, and as if he, on his side, was saying something that no one else must hear. Then, spying the plate of cherries, he pretended to seize it and carry it off by stealth, running away towards Sonia, and dropping on the grass under the linden-tree in the midst of her accumulation of dolls. Sonia was about to fly into a little rage, but he made peace with her by proposing a new game, the point of which lay in seeing which of the two could devour the most cherries.

"Shall I order some more?" I asked, "or shall we go gather them for ourselves?"

He picked up the plate, piled Sonia's dolls in it, and we all three started for the cherry orchard. Sonia, shouting with laughter, trotted after him, tugging at his coat to make him give her back her family. He did so; and turning gravely to me:

"Come, how can you convince me that you are not a violet?" he said, still speaking very low, though there was now no one for him to be afraid of waking; "as soon as I came near you, after having been through so much dust and heat and fatigue, I seemed to perceive the fragrance of a violet, not, it is true, that violet with the powerful perfume, but the little early one, you know, which steals out first, still modest, to breathe at once the expiring snow and the springing grass...."

"But, tell me, is the harvest coming on well?" I put in hastily, to cover the happy confusion his words caused me.

"Wonderfully! what excellent people these all are,—the more one knows them, the more one loves them."

"Oh, yes!—A little while ago, before you came, I sat watching their work, and it really went to my conscience to see them toiling so faithfully, while I was just idly taking my ease, and...."

"Do not play with these sentiments, Katia," he interrupted, with a serious manner, giving me at the same time a caressing glance, "there is holy work there. May God guard you from *posing* in such matters!"

"But it was only to you that I said that!"

"I know it.—Well, and our cherries?"

The cherry orchard was locked, not a single gardener was to be found (he had sent them all to the harvest fields). Sonia ran off to look for the key; but, without waiting for her return, he climbed up at a corner by catching hold of the meshes of the net, and jumped down inside the wall.

"Will you give me the plate?" he asked me, from within.

"No, I want to gather some, myself; I will go get the key, I doubt if Sonia can find it."

But at that moment a sudden fancy seized me, to find out what he was doing there, how he looked, in short his demeanor when he supposed no one could see him. Or rather, honestly, perhaps just then I did not feel like losing sight of him for a single instant. So on my tip-toes, through the nettles, I made a circuit around the little orchard and gained the opposite side, where the enclosure was lower; there, stepping up on an empty tub, I found the wall but breast-high, and leaned over. I made a survey of everything within; looked at the crooked old trees, the large serrated leaves, the black, vertical clusters of juicy fruit; and, slipping my head under the net, I could observe Sergius Mikaïlovitch through the twisted boughs of an old cherry-tree. He was certainly confident that I had gone, and that no one could see him.

With bared head and closed eyes he was sitting on the mouldering trunk of an old tree, absently rolling between his fingers a bit of cherry-gum. All at once, he opened his eyes, and murmured something, with a smile. The word and smile were so little in keeping with what I knew of him that I was ashamed of having watched him. It really seemed to me that the word was: Katia! "That cannot be!" I said to myself. "Dear Katia!" he repeated lower, and still more tenderly. And this time I heard the two words distinctly. My heart began to beat so fast, I was so filled with joyful emotion, I even felt, as it were, such a kind of shock, that I had to hold on to the wall with both hands, to keep myself from falling, and so betraying myself. He heard my movement, and glanced behind him, startled; then suddenly casting down his eyes he blushed, reddening like a child. He made an effort to speak to me, but could not, and this failure made his face grow deeper and deeper scarlet. Yet he smiled as he looked at me. I smiled at him too. He looked all alive with happiness; this was no longer, then,—oh, no, this *was* no longer an old uncle lavishing cares and caresses upon me; I had there before my eyes a man on my own level, loving me and fearing me; a man whom I myself feared, and loved. We did not speak, we only looked at each other. But suddenly he bent his brows darkly; smile and glow went out of his eyes simultaneously, and his bearing became again cold and fatherly, as if we had been doing something wrong, as if he had regained control of himself and was counselling me to do the same.

"Get down from there, you will hurt yourself," said he. "And arrange your hair; you ought to see what you look like!"

"Why does he dissemble so? Why does he wish to wound me?" I thought, indignantly. And at the moment came an irresistible desire to move him again, and to try my power over him.

"No, I want to gather some cherries, myself," I said; and grasping a neighboring bough with my hands, I swung myself over the wall. He had no time to catch me, I dropped to the ground in the middle of the little space.

"What folly is this?" he exclaimed, flushing again, and endeavoring to conceal his alarm under a semblance of anger. "You might injure yourself! And how are you going to get out?"

He was much more perturbed than when he first caught sight of me; but now this agitation no longer gladdened me, on the contrary it made me afraid. I was attacked by it in my turn; I blushed, moved away, no longer knowing what to say to him, and began to pick cherries very fast, without having anything to put them in. I reproached myself, I repented, I was frightened, it seemed to me that by this step I had ruined myself forever in his eyes. We both remained speechless, and the silence weighed heavily upon both. Sonia, running back with the key, freed us from our embarrassing situation. However, we still persistently avoided speaking to each other, both preferring to address little Sonia instead. When we were again with Macha, (who vowed she had not been asleep, and had heard everything that had gone on,) my calmness returned, while he, on his side, made another effort to resume his tone of paternal kindness. But the effort was not successful, and did not deceive me at all. A certain conversation that had taken place two days before still lived in my memory.

Macha had announced her opinion that a man loves more easily than a woman, and also more easily expresses his love. She added:

"A man can say that he loves, and a woman cannot."

"Now it seems to me that a man neither ought nor can say that he loves," was his reply.

I asked him why.

"Because it would always be a lie. What is this discovery that a man *loves*? As if he had only to pronounce the word, and there must immediately spring from it something extraordinary, some phenomenon or other, exploding all at once! It seems to me that those people who say to you solemnly: 'I love you,' either deceive themselves, or, which is worse, deceive others."

"Then you think a woman is to know that she is loved, without being told?" asked Macha.

"That I do not know; every man has his own fashion of speech. But such feelings make themselves understood. When I read a novel, I always try to imagine the embarrassed air of Lieutenant Crelski or Alfred, as he declares: 'Eléonore, I love thee!' which speech he fancies is going to produce something astounding, all of a sudden,—while in reality it causes nothing at all, neither in her nor in him: features, look, everything, remain precisely the same!"

He spoke jestingly, but I thought I detected an undertone of serious meaning, which might have some reference to me; and Macha never allowed even playful aspersions upon her heroes of romance.

"Always paradoxes!" she exclaimed. "Come now, be honest, have you yourself never said to a woman that you loved her?"

"Never have I said so, never have I bowed a knee," he replied laughing, "and never will I!"

"Yes, he need not tell me that he loves me!" I thought, now vividly recalling this conversation. "He does love me, and I know it. And all his efforts to seem indifferent cannot take away this conviction!"

During the whole evening he said very little to me, but in every word, in every look and motion, I felt love, and no longer had any doubts. The only thing that vexed and troubled me was that he should still judge it necessary to conceal this feeling, and to feign coldness, when already all was so clear, and we might have been so easily and so frankly happy almost beyond the verge of possibility. Then, too, I was tormenting myself as though I had committed a crime, for having jumped down into the cherry orchard to join him, and it seemed as if he must have ceased to esteem me, and must feel resentment against me.

After tea, I went to the piano, and he followed.

"Play something, Katia, I have not heard you for a long time," he said, joining me in the drawing-room. "I wished ... Sergius Mikaïlovitch!" And suddenly I looked right into his eyes. "You are not angry with me?"

"Why should I be?"

"Because I did not obey you this afternoon," said I, blushing.

He understood me, shook his head, and smiled. And this smile said that perhaps he would willingly have scolded me a little, but had no longer the strength to do so.

"That is done with, then, isn't it? And we are good friends again?" I asked, seating myself at the piano.

"I think so, indeed!"

The large, lofty apartment was lighted, only by the two candles upon the piano, and the greater portion of it was in semi-darkness; through the open windows we beheld the luminous stillness of the summer night. The most perfect calm reigned, only broken at intervals by Macha's footfall in the adjoining room, which was not yet lighted, or by an occasional restless snort or stamp from our visitor's horse, which was tied under one of the casements. Sergius Mikaïlovitch was seated behind me, so that I could not see him, but in the imperfect darkness of the room, in the soft notes that filled it, in the very depths of my being, I seemed to feel his presence. Every look, every movement, though I could not distinguish them, seemed to enter and echo in my heart. I was playing Mozart's Caprice-sonata, which he had brought me, and which I had learned before him and for him. I was not thinking at all of what I played, but I found that I was playing well and thought he was pleased. I shared his enjoyment, and without seeing him, I knew that from his place his eyes were fixed on me. By a quite involuntary movement, while my fingers continued to run over the keys, unconscious of what they were doing, I turned and looked at him; his head stood out in dark relief against the luminous background of the night. He was sitting with his brow resting on his hand, watching me attentively with sparkling eyes. As mine met them, I smiled, and stopped playing. He smiled also, and made a motion with his head towards my notes, as if reproaching me and begging me to keep on. Just then the moon, midway in her course, soared in full splendor from a light cloud, pouring into the room waves of silvery radiance which overcame the feeble gleam of our wax candles, and swept in a sea of glory over the inlaid floor. Macha said that what I had done was like nothing at all, that I had stopped at the very loveliest part, and that, besides, I had played miserably; he, on the contrary, insisted that I had never succeeded better than this evening, and began pacing about restlessly, from the dim drawing-room into the hall, from the hall back again into the drawing-room, and every time he passed he looked at me and smiled. I smiled too though without any reason; I wanted to laugh, so happy was I at what had taken place that day, at that moment even. While the door hid him from me for an instant I pounced upon Macha and began to kiss her in my pet place on her soft throat under her chin, but when he reappeared I was perfectly grave, although it was hard work to keep from laughing.

"What has happened to her, to-day?" Macha said.

He made no answer, but began to tease and make laughing conjectures. He knew well enough what had happened to me!

"Just see what a night!" he said presently, from the door of the drawing-room, opening on the garden balcony.

We went and stood by him, and indeed I never remember such a night. The full moon shone down upon us from above the house with a glory I have never seen in her since; the long shadows of the roof, of the slender columns and tent-shaped awning of the terrace stretched out in oblique foreshortening, over the gravel walk and part of the large oval of turf. The rest lay in brilliant light, glistening with dew-drops turned by the moon's rays to liquid silver. A wide path, bordered with flowers, was diagonally cut into at one edge by the shadows of tall dahlias and their supporting stakes, and then ran on, an unbroken band of white light and gleaming pebbles until it was lost in the mist of distance. The glass roof of the orangery sparkled through the trees, and a soft vapor stealing up the sides of the ravine grew denser every moment. The tufts of lilac, now partially faded, were pierced through and through by the light; every slender foot-stalk was visible, and the tiny flowers, freshened by the dew, could easily be distinguished from each other. In the paths light and shadow were so blended that one would no longer have said there were trees and paths, but transparent edifices shaken with soft vibrations. On the right of the house all was obscure, indistinct, almost a horror of darkness. But out of it sprang, more resplendent from the black environment, the fantastic head of a poplar which, by some strange freak, ended abruptly close above the house in an aureole of clear light, instead of rising to lose itself in the distant depths of dark blue sky.

"Let us go to walk," said I.

Macha consented, but added that I must put on my galoshes.

"It is not necessary," I said; "Sergius Mikaïlovitch will give me his arm."

As if that could keep me from getting my feet wet! But at that moment, to each of us three, such absurdity was admissible, and caused no astonishment. He had never given me his arm, and now I took it of my own accord, and he did not seem surprised. We all three descended to the terrace. The whole universe, the sky, the garden, the air we breathed, no longer appeared to me what I had always known.

As I looked ahead of me in the path we were pursuing, I began to fancy that one could not go beyond, that there the possible world ended, and that all there would abide forever in its present loveliness.

However, as we went on, this enchanted wall, this barrier built of pure beauty, receded before us and yielded us passage, and I found myself in the midst of familiar objects, garden, trees, paths, dry leaves. These were certainly real paths that we were pursuing, where we crossed alternate spaces of light and spheres of darkness, where the dry leaves rustled beneath our feet, and the dewy sprays softly touched my cheek as we passed. It was really he, who walked by my side with slow, steady steps and with distant formality, allowed my arm to rest upon his own. It was the real moon, high in the heavens, whose light came down to us through the motionless branches.

Once I looked at him. There was only a single linden in the part of the path we were then following, and I could see his face clearly. He was so handsome; he looked so happy....

He was saying: "Are you not afraid?" But the words I heard, were: "I love thee, dear child! I love thee! I love thee!" His look said it, and his arm said it; the light, the shadow, the air, and all things repeated it.

We went through the whole garden, Macha walked near us, taking short steps, and panting a little, she was so tired. She said it was time to go in, and I was so sorry for the poor creature. "Why does not she feel like us?" I thought. "Why is not everybody always young and happy? How full this night is of youth and happiness,—and we too!"

We returned to the house, but it was a long time before Sergius Mikaïlovitch went away. Macha forgot to remind us that it was late; we talked of all sorts of things, perhaps trivial enough, sitting side by side without the least suspicion that it was three o'clock in the morning. The cocks had crowed for the third time, before he went. He took leave of us as usual, not saying anything particular. But I could not doubt that from this day he was mine, and I could no longer lose him. Now that I recognized that I loved him, I told Macha all. She was delighted and touched, but the poor woman got no sleep that night; and as for me, after walking a long, long time up and down the terrace, I went to the garden again, seeking to recall every word, every incident, as I wandered through the paths where we had so lately passed together. I did not go to bed, that night, and, for the first time in my life, I saw the sun rise and knew what the dawn of day is. Never again have I seen such a night and such a morning. But I still kept asking myself why he did not tell me frankly that he loved me. "Why," thought I, "does he invent such or such difficulties, why does he consider himself old, when everything is so simple and so beautiful? Why lose thus a precious time which perhaps will never return? Let him say that he loves, let him say it in words, let him take my hand in his, bend down his head and say: "I love." Let his face flush, and his eyes fall before me, and then I will tell him all. Or, rather, I will tell him nothing, I will only hold him fast in my arms and let my tears flow. But if I am mistaken?—if he does not love me?" This thought suddenly crossed my mind.

I was terrified by my own feeling. Heaven knows where it might have led me; already the memory of his confusion and my own when I suddenly dropped down into the cherry orchard beside him, weighed upon me, oppressed my heart. The tears filled my eyes, and I began to pray. Then a thought, a strange thought, came to me, which brought me a great quietness, and rekindled my hope. This was, the resolution to commence my devotions, and to choose my birthday as my betrothal day.

How and why? How could it come to pass? That I knew nothing about,—but from this moment I believed that it would be so. In the meantime, broad day had come, and every one was rising as I returned to my chamber.

CHAPTER-IV

IT was the *Carême de l'Assomption,*[C] and consequently no one was surprised at my commencing a season of devotion.

During this whole week Sergius Mikaïlovitch did not once come to see us, and far from being surprised, alarmed, or angry with him, I was content, and did not expect him before my birthday. Throughout this week I rose very early every day, and while the horses were being harnessed I walked in the garden, alone, meditating upon the past, and thinking what I must do in order that the evening should find me satisfied with my day, and proud of having committed no faults.

When the horses were ready, I entered the droschky, accompanied by Macha or a maid-servant, and drove about three versts to church. In entering the church, I never failed to remember that we pray there for all those "who enter this place in the fear of God," and I strove to rise to the level of this thought, above all when my feet first touched the two grass-grown steps of the porch. At this hour there were not usually in the church more than ten or a dozen persons, peasants and droroviés, preparing to make their devotions; I returned their salutations with marked humility, and went myself, (which I regarded as an act of superior merit,) to the drawer where the wax tapers were kept, received a few from the hand of the old soldier who performed the office of staroste,[D] and placed them before the images. Through the door of the sanctuary I could see the altar-cloth Mamma had embroidered, and above the iconstase[E] two angels spangled with stars, which I had considered magnificent when I was a little girl; and a dove surrounded by a gilded aureole which, at that same period, often used to absorb

[C] This expression, peculiar to Russia, corresponds to what in Catholic countries is called: Making a preparatory retreat.

[D] In the Greek Church the staroste acts as church-warden, collector of alms, *etc.*

[E] Screen, upon which are the images.

my attention. Behind the choir I caught a glimpse of the embossed fonts near which I had so often held the children of our drorovíés, and where I myself had received baptism. The old priest appeared, wearing a chasuble cut from cloth which had been the pall of my father's coffin, and he intoned the service in the same voice which, as far back as I could remember, had chanted the offices of the Church at our house, at Sonia's baptism, at my father's funeral service, at my mother's burial. In the choir I heard the familiar cracked voice of the precentor; I saw, as I had always seen her, a certain old woman, almost bent double, who came to every service, leaned her back against the wall, and, holding her faded handkerchief in her tightly clasped hands, gazed with eyes full of tears at one of the images in the choir, mumbling I knew not what prayers with her toothless mouth. And all these objects, all these beings,—it was not mere curiosity or reminiscence which brought them so near to me; all seemed in my eyes great and holy, all were full of profound meaning.

I lent an attentive ear to every word of the prayers I heard read, I endeavored to bring my feelings into accord with them, and if I did not comprehend them, I mentally besought God to enlighten me, or substituted a petition of my own for that which I had not understood. When the penitential prayers were read, I recalled my past, and this past of my innocent childhood appeared to me so black in comparison with the state of serenity in which my soul was, at this time, that I wept over myself, terrified; yet I felt that all was forgiven me, and that even if I had had many more faults to reproach myself with, repentance would only have been all the sweeter to me.

At the conclusion of the service, at the moment when the priest pronounced the words: "May the blessing of the Lord our God be upon you," I seemed to feel within me, instantaneously communicated to all my being, a sense of even, as it were, physical comfort, as if a current of light and warmth had suddenly poured into my very heart.

When the service was over, if the priest approached me to ask if he should come to our house to celebrate vespers, and what hour would suit me, I thanked him with emotion for his offer, but told him that I would come myself to the church either on foot or in the carriage.

"So you will yourself take that trouble?" he asked.

I could not answer, for fear of sinning from pride. Unless Macha was with me, I sent the carriage home from the church, and returned on foot, alone, saluting humbly all whom I met, seeking occasion to assist them, to advise them, to sacrifice myself for them in some way; helping to lift a load or carry a child, or stepping aside into the mud to yield a passage.

One evening I heard our intendant, in making his report to Macha, say that a peasant, Simon, had come to beg for some wood to make a coffin for his daughter, and for a silver rouble to pay for the mortuary service, and that his request had been complied with.

"Are they so poor?" I enquired.

"Very poor, my lady; they live without salt,"[F] replied the intendant.

I was distressed, yet, at the same time, in a manner rejoiced to hear this. Making Macha believe that I was going for a walk, I ran upstairs, took all my money (it was very little, but it was all I had,) and, having made the sign of the cross, hurried off, across the terrace and garden, to Simon's cottage in the village. It was at the end of the little cluster of houses, and, unseen by anyone, I approached the window, laid the money upon the sill and tapped gently. The door opened, some one came out of the cottage and called to me; but I, cold and trembling with fear like a criminal, ran away home. Macha asked where I had been, what was the matter with me? But I did not even understand what she was saying, and made no reply.

Everything at this moment appeared to me so small, and of so little consequence! I shut myself up in my chamber, and walked up and down there alone, for a long time, not feeling disposed to do anything, to think anything, and incapable of analyzing my own sensations. I imagined the delight of the whole family, and what they would all say about the person who had placed the money upon their window, and I began to regret that I had not given it to them myself. I wondered what Sergius Mikaïlovitch would have said, if he had known what I had done, and I was delighted to think that he never would know it. And I was so seized with joy, so filled with a sense of the imperfection in myself and in all, yet so inclined to view with gentleness all these others, as well as myself, that the thought of death offered itself to me as a vision of bliss. I smiled, I prayed, I wept, and at this instant I suddenly loved every creature in the world, and I loved myself with a strange ardor. Searching my prayer-book, I read many passages from the Gospel, and all that I

[F] Strong Russian phrase, to express great poverty.

read in this volume became more and more intelligible; the story of that divine life, appeared to me more touching and simple, while the depth of feeling and of thought revealed to me, in this reading, became more terrible and impenetrable. And how clear and easy everything seemed, when, on laying aside the book, I looked at my life and meditated upon it. It seemed impossible not to live aright, and very simple to love every one and to be loved by every one. Besides, every one was good and gentle to me, even Sonia, whom I continued to teach, and who had become totally different, who really made an effort to understand, and to satisfy me, and give me no annoyance. What I was trying to be to others, others were to me.

Passing then to my enemies, from whom I must obtain forgiveness before the great day, I could not think of any except one young lady in the neighborhood, whom I had laughed at before some company, about a year before, and who had ceased to visit at our house. I wrote a letter to her, acknowledging my fault, and begging her pardon. She responded by fully granting it, and asking mine in return. I shed tears of pleasure while reading these frank lines, which seemed to me full of deep and touching sentiment. My maid wept when I asked her pardon also. Why were they all so good to me? How had I deserved so much affection? I asked myself. Involuntarily I began to think about Sergius Mikaïlovitch. I could not help it, and besides I did not consider it a light or frivolous diversion. True I was not thinking about him at all as I had done on that night when, for the first time, I found out that I loved him; I was thinking of him just as of myself, linking him, in spite of myself, with every plan and idea of my future. The dominating influence which his presence had exercised over me, faded away completely in my imagination. I felt myself to-day his equal, and, from the summit of the ideal edifice whence I was looking down, I had full comprehension of him. Whatever in him had previously appeared strange to me was now intelligible. To-day, for the first time, I could appreciate the thought he had expressed to me, that happiness consists in living for others, and to-day I felt in perfect unison with him. It appeared to me that we two were to enjoy a calm and illimitable happiness. No thought entered my mind of journeys to foreign lands, guests at home, excitement, stir, and gayety; it was to be a peaceful existence, a home life in the country, perpetual abnegation of one's own will, perpetual love for each other, perpetual and absolute thankfulness to a loving and helpful Providence.

I concluded my devotions, as I had purposed, upon the anniversary of my birth. My heart was so overflowing with happiness, that day, when I returned from church, that there resulted all kinds of dread of life, fear of every feeling, terrors of whatever might disturb this happiness. But we had scarcely descended from the droschky to the steps before the house, when I heard the well-known sound of his cabriolet upon the bridge, and in a moment Sergius Mikaïlovitch was with us. He offered me his congratulations, and we went into the drawing-room together. Never since I had known him, had I found myself so calm, so independent in his presence, as upon this morning. I felt that I bore within myself an entire new world, which he did not comprehend and which was superior to him. I did not feel the least agitation in his society. He may, however, have understood what was passing within me, for his gentleness to me was peculiarly delicate, almost, as it were, a religious deference. I was going towards the piano, but he locked it and put the key in his pocket, saying:

"Do not spoil the state of mind I see you are in; there is sounding, at this moment, in the depths of your soul, a music which no harmony of this earth can approach!"

I was grateful to him for this thought, yet, at the same time, it was a little displeasing to me that he should thus understand, too easily, and too clearly, what was to remain secret from all, in the kingdom of my soul.

After dinner he said that he had come to bring me his congratulations and to say farewell, as he was going to Moscow on the following day. He was looking at Macha when he said this, but he gave me a quick side-glance as if he was afraid of noticing some emotion upon my countenance. But I showed neither surprise nor agitation, and did not even ask if his absence would be long. I knew that he said so, but I knew that he was not going. How? I cannot, now, explain it in the least; but on this memorable day it appeared to me that I knew all that had been, and all that would be. I was in a mood akin to one of those happy dreams, where one has a kind of luminous vision of both the future and the past.

He had intended going immediately after dinner, but Macha had left the table, to take her siesta, and he was obliged to wait until she awoke in order to take leave of her.

The sun was shining full into the drawing-room, and we went out upon the terrace. We were scarcely seated, when I entered upon the conversation which was to decide the fate of my love. I began to speak, neither sooner nor later, but at the first moment that found us face to face alone, when nothing else had been said, when nothing had stolen into the tone and general character of the conversation which might hinder or embarrass what I wished to say. I cannot myself comprehend whence came the calmness, the resolution, the precision of my words. One would have said that it was not I who was talking, and that something—I know not what—independent of my own volition, was making me speak. He was seated opposite to me, and, having drawn down to him a branch of lilac, began to pluck off its leaves. When I opened my lips, he let go the little branch, and covered his face with his hand. This might be the attitude of a man who was perfectly calm, or that of a man yielding to great agitation.

"Why are you going away?" I began, in a resolute tone; then stopped, and looked him straight in the eyes.

He did not reply at once.

"Business!" he articulated, looking down on the ground.

I saw that it was difficult for him to dissemble in answering a question I put so frankly.

"Listen," said I, "you know what this day is to me. In many ways it is a great day. If I question you, it is not only to show my interest in you (you know I am used to you, and fond of you), I question you because I must know. Why are you going away?"

"It is excessively difficult to tell you the truth, to tell you why I am going away. During this week I have thought a great deal of you and of myself, and I have decided that it is necessary for me to go. You understand ... why? And if you love me, do not question me!"

He passed his hand across his brow, and, covering his eyes again with the same hand, he added:

"This is painful to me.... But you understand, Katia!"

My heart began to beat hard in my breast.

"I cannot understand," said I, "*I cannot do it*; but *you*, speak to me, in the name of God, in the name of this day, speak to me, I can hear everything calmly."

He changed his attitude, looked at me, and caught the branch of lilac again.

"Well," he resumed, after a moment's silence, in a voice which vainly struggled to appear firm, "though it may be absurd, and almost impossible to translate into words, and though it will cost me much, I will try to explain to you;"—and as he uttered the words there were lines on his brow, as if he was suffering physical pain.

"Go on," I said.

"You must suppose there is a gentleman,—A. we will call him,—old, weary of existence; and a lady,—Madame B. we will say,—young, happy, and as yet knowing neither the world nor life. In consequence of family relations A. loved B. like a daughter, with no fear of coming to love her differently."

He was silent, and I did not interrupt him.

"But," he suddenly pursued, in a brief, resolute voice, without looking at me, "he had forgotten that B. was young, that for her life was still but a game, that it might easily happen that he might love her, and that B. might amuse herself with him. He deceived himself, and one fine day he found that another feeling, weighty to bear as remorse, had stolen into his soul, and he was startled. He dreaded to see their old friendly relations thus compromised, and he decided to go away before these had time to change their nature."

As he spoke, he again with seeming carelessness passed his hand across his eyes, and covered them.

"And why did he fear to love differently?" I said, presently, in a steady voice, controlling my emotion; but no doubt this seemed to him mere playful banter, for he answered with the air of a deeply wounded man:

"You are young; I am no longer so. Playing may please you, for me more is necessary. Only, do not play with me, for I assure you it will do me no good,—and you might find it weigh on your conscience! That is what A. said," he added,—"but all this is nonsense; you understand, now, why I am going; let us say no more about it, I beg you...."

"Yes, yes, let us speak of it!" said I, and tears made my voice tremble. "Did she love him or not?"

He did not reply.

"And if he did not love her," I continued, "why did he play with her as if she were a child?"

"Yes, yes, A. had been culpable," he replied interrupting me; "but all that is over, and they have parted from each other ... good friends!"

"But this is frightful! And is there no other end?" I exclaimed, terrified at what I was saying.

"Yes, there is one." And he uncovered his agitated face, and looked at me steadily. "There are even two other ends, quite different. But, for the love of God, do not interrupt me, and listen to me quietly. Some say," he went on, rising, and giving a forced, sad smile, "some say that A. went mad, that he loved B. with an insane love, and that he told her so.... But that she only laughed at him. For her the matter had been but a jest, a trifle; for him,—the one thing in his life!"

I shivered, and would have broken in, to tell him that he should not dare to speak for me; but he stopped me, and, laying his hand upon mine:

"Wait!" he said, in a shaking voice: "others say that she was sorry for him, that she fancied—poor little girl, knowing nothing of the world—that she might actually love him, and that she consented to be his wife. And he—madman—he believed,—believed that all his life was beginning again; but she herself became conscious that she was deceiving him and that he was deceiving her.... Let us talk no more about it!" he concluded, indeed evidently incapable of farther speech, and he silently sat down again opposite me.

He had said, "Let us talk no more about it," but it was manifest that with all the strength of his soul he was waiting for a word from me. Indeed I tried to speak, and could not; something stopped my breath. I looked at him, he was pale, and his lower lip was trembling. I was very sorry for him. I made another effort, and suddenly succeeding in breaking the silence which paralyzed me. I said, in a slow, concentrated voice, fearing every moment it would fail me:

"There is a third end to the story" (I stopped, but he remained silent), "and this other end is that he did not love her, that he hurt her, hurt her cruelly, that he believed he was right to do it, that he ... that he went away, and that, moreover, moreover, he was proud of it. It is not on my side, but on yours, that the trifling has been, from the first day I loved you; I loved you," I repeated, and at the word "loved" my voice involuntarily changed from its tone of slow concentration to a kind of wild cry which appalled myself.

He was standing up before me, very pale, his lip trembled more and more, and I saw two heavy tears making their way down his cheeks.

“This is dreadful!”—I could barely get out the words, choked with anger and unshed tears.—“And why?...” I jumped up hastily, to run away.

But he sprang towards me. In a moment his head was upon my knees, my trembling hands were pressed again and again to his lips, and I felt hot drops falling upon them.

“My God, if I had known!” he was murmuring.

“Why? why?” I repeated mechanically, my soul in the grasp of that transport which seizes, possesses, and flies forever, that rapture which returns no more.

Five minutes afterwards, Sonia went dashing upstairs to Macha, and all over the house, crying out that Katia was going to marry Sergius Mikaïlovitch.

CHAPTER-V

THERE was no reason to delay our marriage, and neither he nor I desired to do so. It is true that Macha longed to go to Moscow to order my trousseau, and Sergius' mother considered it incumbent upon him before marrying to buy a new carriage and more furniture and have the whole house renovated, but we both insisted that this could all be done quite as well afterwards, and that we would be married at the end of the fortnight succeeding my birthday, without trousseau, parade, guests, groomsmen, supper, champagne, or any of the traditional attributes of a wedding. He told me that his mother was unwilling to have the great event take place without the music, the avalanche of trunks, the refurnished house, which, at a cost of thirty thousand roubles, had accompanied her own marriage; and how, without his knowledge, she had ransacked for treasures all the chests in the lumber rooms, and held sober consultations with Mariouchka, the housekeeper, on the subject of certain new carpets and curtains, quite indispensable to our happiness. On our side, Macha was similarly employed, with my maid Kouzminicha. She could not be laughed out of this; being firmly persuaded that when Sergius and I ought to have been discussing our future arrangements, we wasted our time in soft speeches (as was perhaps natural in our position); while of course, in fact, the very substance of our future happiness was dependent upon the cut and embroidery of my dresses, and the straight hems on our table-cloths and napkins. Between Pokrovski and Nikolski, every day and several times a day, mysterious communications were exchanged as to the progressing preparations; and though apparently Macha and the bridegroom's mother were upon the tenderest terms, one felt sure of the constant passage of shafts of keen and hostile diplomacy between the two powers.

Tatiana Semenovna, his mother, with whom I now became more fully acquainted, was a woman of the old school, starched and stiff, and a severe mistress. Sergius loved her, not only from duty as a son, but also with the sentiment of a man who saw in her the best, the most intelligent, the tenderest, and the most amiable woman in the world. Tatiana had always been cordial and kind to us, particularly to me, and she was delighted that her son should marry; but as soon as I became betrothed to him it appeared to me that she wished to make me feel that he might have made a better match, and that I ought never to forget the fact. I perfectly understood her, and was entirely of her opinion.

During these last two weeks, Sergius and I saw each other every day; he always dined with us and remained until midnight; but, though he often told me—and I knew he was telling the truth—that he could not now live without me, yet he never spent the whole day with me, and even, after a fashion, continued to attend to his business matters. Our outward relations, up to the very time of our marriage, were exactly what they had been; we still said "*you*" to each other, he did not even kiss my hand, and not only did he not seek, but he actually avoided occasions of finding himself alone with me, as if he feared giving himself up too much to the great and dangerous love he bore in his heart.

All these days the weather was bad, and we spent most of them in the drawing-room; our conversations being held in the corner between the piano and the window.

"Do you know that there is one thing I have been wishing to say to you for a long time?" he said, late one evening, when we were alone in our corner. "I have been thinking of it, all the time you have been at the piano."

"Tell me nothing, I know all," I replied.

"Well then, we will say no more about it."

"Oh, yes, indeed, tell me; what is it?" I asked.

"It is this. You remember me telling you that story about A. and B.?"

"As if I could help remembering that foolish story! How lucky that it has ended so...."

"A little more, and I would have destroyed my happiness with my own hand; you saved me; but the thing is, that I was not truthful with you, then; it has been on my conscience, and now I wish to tell you all."

"Ah, please do not!"

"Do not be afraid," he said, smiling, "it is only that I must justify myself. When I began to talk to you, I wished to debate the question."

"Why debate?" said I, "that is never necessary."

He looked at me in silence, then went on.

"In regard to the end of that story,—what I said to you, then, was not nonsense; clearly there was something to fear, and I was right to fear it. To receive everything from you, and give you so little! You are yet a child, yet an unexpanded flower, you love for the first time, while I...."

"Oh, yes, tell me the truth!" I exclaimed. But all at once I was afraid of his answer. "No, do not tell me!" I added.

"Whether I have loved before? is that it?" he said, instantly divining my thought. "It is easy to tell you that. No, I have not loved. Never has such a feeling.... So, do you not see how imperative it was for me to reflect, before telling you that I loved you? What am I giving you? Love, it is true...."

"Is that so little?" I asked, looking into his face.

"Yes, that is little, my darling, little for you. You have beauty and youth. Often, at night, I cannot sleep for happiness; I am incessantly thinking how we are going to live together. I have already lived much, yet it seems to me that I have but just now come to the knowledge of what makes happiness. A sweet, tranquil life, in our retired corner, with the possibility of doing good to those to whom it is so easy to do it, and who, nevertheless, are so little used to it; then work,—work, whence, you know, some profit always springs; recreation, also, nature, books, music, the affection of some congenial friend; there is my happiness, a happiness higher than I ever dreamed of. And beyond all that, a loved one like you, perhaps a family; in one word, all that a man can desire in this world!"

"Yes," said I.

"For me, whose youth is done, yes; but for you ..." he continued. "You have not yet lived; perhaps you might have wished to pursue your happiness in some other path, and in some other path perhaps you might have found it. At present it seems to you that what I speak of is indeed happiness, because you love me...."

"No, I have never desired nor liked any but this sweet home life. And you have just said precisely what I think, myself."

He smiled.

"It seems so to you, my darling. But that is little for you. You have beauty and youth," he repeated, thoughtfully.

I was beginning to feel provoked at seeing that he would not believe me, and that in a certain way he was reproaching me with my beauty and my youth.

"Come now, why do you love me?" I asked, rather hotly: "for my youth or for myself?"

"I do not know, but I do love," he replied, fixing upon me an observant look, full of alluring sweetness.

I made no response, but involuntarily met his eyes. All at once, a strange thing happened to me. I ceased to see what was around me, his face itself disappeared from before me, and I could distinguish nothing but the fire of the eyes exactly opposite mine; then it seemed to me that these eyes themselves were piercing into me, then all became confused, I could no longer see anything at all, and I was obliged to half close my eyelids to free myself from the mingled sensation of joy and terror produced by this look.

Towards evening of the day previous to that appointed for our marriage, the weather cleared. After the heavy continuous rains of the summer we had the first brilliant autumnal sunset. The sky was pure, rigid, and pale. I went to sleep, happy in the thought that the next day would be bright, for our wedding. I woke in the morning with the sun upon me, and with the thought that here already was the day ... as if it astonished and frightened me. I went to the garden. The sun had just risen, and was shining through the linden-trees, whose yellow leaves were floating down and strewing the paths. There was not one cloud to be seen in the cold serene sky.

"Is it possible that it is to-day?" I asked myself, not venturing to believe in my own happiness. "Is it possible that to-morrow I shall not wake here, that I shall open my eyes in that house of Nikolski, with its columns, in a place now all strange to me! Is it possible that henceforward I shall not be expecting him, shall not be going to meet him, shall not talk about him any more in the evenings, with Macha? Shall I no longer sit at the piano in our drawing-room at Pokrovski, with him beside me? Shall I no longer see him go away, and tremble with fear for him because the night is dark?" But I remembered that he had told me, the night before, that it was his last visit; and, besides, Macha had made me try on my wedding-dress. So that, by moments, I would believe, and then doubt again. Was it really true that this very day I was to begin to live with a mother-in-law, without Nadine, without old Gregory, without Macha? That at night

I would not embrace my old nurse, and hear her say, making the sign of the cross, as she always did; "Good-night, my young lady?" That I would no longer hear Sonia's lessons, or play with her, or rap on the partition wall in the morning and hear her gay laugh? Was it possible that it was really to-day that I was to become, in a measure, an alien to myself, and that a new life, realizing my hopes and my wishes, was opening before me? And was it possible that this new life, just beginning, was to be for ever? I waited impatiently for Sergius, so hard it was for me to remain alone with these thoughts. He came early, and it was only when he was actually there that I was sure that to-day I was really going to be his wife, and no longer felt frightened at the thought.

Before dinner we went to church, to hear the service for the dead, in commemoration of my father.

"Oh, if he were still in this world!" thought I, as I was returning home, leaning silently on the arm of the man who had been his dearest friend. While the prayers were being read, kneeling with my brow pressed upon the cold flag-stones of the chapel floor, my father had been so vividly brought before my mind, that I could not help believing that he comprehended me and blessed my choice, and I imagined that, at the moment, his soul was hovering above us, and that his benediction rested upon me. These remembrances, these hopes, my happiness and my regrets, blended within me into a feeling at once solemn and sweet, which seemed, as it were, to be set in a frame of clear quiet air, stillness, bare fields, pale heavens whose brilliant but enfeebled rays vainly strove to bring the color to my cheek. I persuaded myself that my companion was understanding and sharing my feelings. He walked with slow steps, in silence, and his face, which I glanced into from time to time, bore the impress of that intense state of the soul, which is neither sadness nor joy, and which perfectly harmonized with surrounding nature and with my heart.

All at once, he turned towards me, and I saw that he had something to say to me. What if he were not going to speak of what was in my thoughts? But without even naming him he spoke of my father, and added:

"One day he happened to say to me, laughingly, 'You will marry my little Katia!'"

"How glad he would have been, to-day," I responded, pressing closer to the arm on which I leaned.

"Yes, you were then but a child," he went on, looking deep into my eyes; "I kissed those eyes and loved them simply because they were so like his, and I was far from thinking that one day they would be so dear to me in themselves."

We were still walking slowly along the field-path, scarcely traceable among the trodden and scattered stubble, and heard no sound save our own footsteps and voices. The sun poured down floods of light that gave no warmth. When we spoke, our voices seemed to resound and hang suspended above our heads in the motionless atmosphere. We might have thought we two were alone upon the earth, alone beneath that blue vault vibrating with cold scintillations from the sun.

When we arrived at the house, we found his mother already there, with the few guests whom we had felt obliged to invite, and I was not again alone with him until we had left the church and were in the carriage on our way to Nikolski.

The church had been almost empty. At one glance I had seen his mother, standing near the choir; Macha, with her wet cheeks and lilac cap-ribbons; and two or three *drorovies*, who were gazing at me with curious eyes. I heard the prayers, I repeated them, but they had no meaning for me. I could not pray, myself, I only kept looking stupidly at the images, the wax tapers, the cross embroidered on the chasuble the priest had on, the iconostase, the church windows, but did not seem able to understand anything at all; I only felt that something very extraordinary was being done to me. When the priest turned towards us with the cross, when he gave us his congratulations, and said that he had baptized me and that now God had permitted him also to marry me; when Macha and Sergius' mother embraced us, when I heard Gregory's voice calling the carriage, I was astonished and frightened at the thought that all was finished, though no marvellous change, corresponding with the sacrament which had just been performed over me, had taken place in my soul. We kissed each other, and this kiss appeared to me so odd, so out of keeping with ourselves, that I could not help thinking: "It is only *that*?" We went out upon the parvise, the noise of the wheels echoed loudly within the arch of the church; I felt the fresh air upon my face, and was conscious that, Sergius with his hat under his arm, had assisted me into the carriage. Through the window I saw that the moon was shining in her place in the frosty sky. He took his seat beside me, and shut the door. Something, at this moment, seemed to strike through my heart, as if the assurance with which he did this had given me a wound. The wheels glanced against a stone, then began to revolve upon the smooth road, and we were gone. Drawn back into a corner of the carriage, I watched the fields flooded with light, and the flying road. Nevertheless, without looking at him, I was feeling that there he was, beside me. "Here, then, is all that this first moment from which I have expected so much, brings me?" I thought, and all at once I had a sense of humiliation and offence at finding myself seated thus alone with him and so close to him. I turned towards him, intending to say something, no matter what. But no word would come from my lips; one would have said that no trace of my former tenderness lingered within my heart, but that it was entirely replaced by this impression of alarm and offence.

"Up to this moment, I still dared not believe that this might be!" he softly responded to my glance. "And I ... I am afraid ... I know not why!"

"Afraid of me, Katia?" he said, taking my hand, and bending his head over it.

My hand rested within his, lifeless; my heart stopped beating.

"Yes," I murmured.

But, at the same moment, my heart suddenly began to beat again, my hand trembled and clasped his, warmth returned to me; my eyes, in the dim light, sought his eyes, and I felt, all at once, that I was no longer afraid of him; that this terror had been but a new love, yet more tender and strong than the old. I knew that I was wholly his, and that I was happy to be wholly in his power.

CHAPTER-VI

THE days, the weeks, two entire months of lonely country life slipped away, imperceptibly, it appeared to us; but the sensations, the emotions, and the happiness of these two months would have sufficed to fill a whole life. My dreams, and his, concerning the mode of organizing our joint existence were not realized exactly as we had anticipated. But, nevertheless, the reality was not below our dreams. This was not the life of strict industry, full of duties, abnegation, and sacrifices, which I had pictured to myself when I became his betrothed; on the contrary, it was the absorbing and egotistical sentiment of love, joys without reason and without end, oblivion of everything in the world. He would, it is true, sometimes retire to his study and occupy himself with something demanding attention; sometimes he went to the city on business, or overlooked his agricultural matters; but I could see how hard it was for him to tear himself away from me. Indeed, he himself said that whenever I was not present, things appeared to him so devoid of interest that the wonder was that he could attend to them at all. It was precisely the same on my side. I read, I busied myself with my music, with Mamma, with the schools; but I only did so because all these employments were in some way connected with him, and met with his approbation, and the instant the thought of him ceased to be in some manner, direct or indirect, associated with anything whatever that I was doing, I would stop doing it. To me, he was the only person in the universe, the handsomest, noblest human being in the wide world; of course, therefore, I could live for nothing but him, could strive for nothing but to remain in his eyes what he considered me. For he honestly considered me the first and highest of women, gifted with every excellence and charm; and my one aim was to be in reality for him this highest and most complete of all existing creatures.

Ours was one of those old country homes, where generation after generation of ancestors had lived, loved each other, and peacefully passed away. The very walls seemed to breathe out happy household memories, and no sooner had I set my foot upon the threshold, than these all appeared to become memories of my own. The arrangement and order of the dwelling were old-fashioned, carefully kept so by Tatiania Semenovna. No one could have said that anything was handsome or elegant, but everything, from the attendance to the furniture and the food, was proper, solid, regular, and seemed to inspire respect. In the drawing-room, tables, chairs, and divans were symmetrically ranged, the walls were hidden by family portraits, and the floor was covered with ancient rugs and immense landscapes in linen. In the small parlor there was an old grand piano, two chiffoniers of different shapes, a divan, and one or two tables decorated with wrought copper. My private room, adorned by Tatiana Semenovna, was honored with all the finest pieces of furniture, irrespective of varying styles and dates, and, among the rest, with an old mirror with doors, which at first I hardly dared to raise my eyes to, but which afterwards became like a dear old friend to me. Tatiana's voice was never heard, but the household went on with the regularity of a well-wound clock, although there were many more servants than were necessary. But all these servants, wearing their soft heelless slippers (for Tatiana Semenovna insisted that creaking soles and pounding heels were, of all things in the world, the most disagreeable), all these servants appeared proud of their condition, trembling before the old lady, showing to my husband and me a protecting good-will, and seeming to take special satisfaction in the discharge of their respective duties. Every Saturday, regularly, the floors were scoured, and the carpets shaken; on the first day of every month, a *Te Deum* was chanted, and holy water sprinkled; while upon every recurring fête-day of Tatiana Semenovna and her son, and now also upon mine (which took place this autumn, for the first time), a feast was given to all the neighborhood. And all this was performed precisely as in the oldest times that Tatiana Semenovna could remember.

My husband interfered in nothing concerning the management of the house, confining himself to the control of the estate, and the affairs of the peasants, which fully occupied him.

He rose very early, even during the winter, so that he was always gone when I woke. He generally returned for tea, which we took alone together; and at these times, having finished the troubles and annoyances of his agricultural matters, he would often fall into that particularly joyous light-hearted state of mind, which we used to call *le transport sauvage*. Often, when I asked him to tell me what he had been doing all the morning, he would relate such perfectly absurd adventures, that we would almost die of laughing; sometimes when I demanded a sober account, he would give it to me, making an effort to restrain even a smile. As for me, I watched his eyes, or the motion of his lips, and did not understand a word he said, being entirely taken up with the pleasure of looking at him and hearing his voice.

"Come, now, what was I saying?" he would ask; "repeat it to me!"

But I never could repeat any of it.

Tatiana Semenovna never made her appearance until dinner time, taking her tea alone, and only sending an ambassador to wish us good-morning. I always found it hard not to burst out laughing, when the maid entered, took her stand before us with her hands crossed one upon the other, and, in her measured tones informed us that Tatiana Semenovna desired to know whether we had slept well, and whether we liked the little cakes we had for tea. Until dinner time we seldom remained together. I played, or read, alone; he wrote, or sometimes went out again; but at four o'clock we went down to the drawing-room for dinner. Mamma came out of her chamber, and then the poor gentle-folk and pilgrims who happened to be lodging in the house, usually two or three in number made their appearance. Regularly every day my husband, following the ancient custom, offered his arm to his mother, to conduct her to the dining-room, and she requested him to take me upon his other arm. Mamma presided at dinner, and the conversation was of a serious, thoughtful turn, not altogether without a shade of solemnity. The simple every-day talk between my husband and myself was the only agreeable diversion in the grave aspect of these table sessions. After dinner, Mamma took her seat in a large arm-chair in the salon, and cut open the leaves of any newly-arrived books; we read aloud, or went to the piano in the small drawing-room. We read a great deal together during those two months, but music continued to be our supreme enjoyment, for every day it seemed to strike some new chord in our hearts, whose vibrations revealed us to each other more and more wholly. When I was playing his favorite airs he retired to a divan at some distance, where I could scarcely see him, and with a kind of modesty of sentiment tried to conceal from me the emotion my music produced; but, often, when he least expected it, I rose from the piano and ran to him, to try to surprise upon his countenance the traces of this deep feeling and to catch the almost supernatural light in the humid eyes which he vainly strove to conceal from me. I presided over our late tea in the large drawing-room, again all the family were gathered round the table, and for a long time this formal assembling near the samovar, as in a tribunal, with the distribution of the cups and glasses, discomposed me very much. It always seemed to me that I was not yet worthy of these honors, that I was too young, too giddy, to turn the faucet of that stately samovar, set the cups on Nikita's tray and say: "For Peter Ivanovitch; for Maria Minichna," and ask: "Is it sweet enough?" And afterwards give out the lumps of sugar for the white-haired nurse and the other old servants. "Perfect, perfect," my husband would often tell me; "quite a grown-up person!" and then I would feel more intimidated than ever.

After tea Mamma played patience, or she and Maria Minichna had a game of cards together; then she embraced us both and gave us her blessing, and we withdrew to our own apartment. There, however, our evening *tête-à-tête* was usually prolonged until midnight, for these were our pleasantest hours in the twenty-four. He told me about his past life, we made plans, occasionally we philosophized, all the time talking in a low tone lest we might be overheard. We lived, he and I, almost upon the footing of strangers in this huge old house, where everything seemed to be weighed upon by the severe spirit of ancient times and of Tatiana Semenovna. Not only she herself, but also the servants, all these old men and women, the furniture, the pictures, all inspired me with respect and a kind of fear, and at the same time with the consciousness that my husband and I were not exactly in our own place there and that our conduct must be extremely circumspect. As well as I remember, now, this severe order and the prodigious number of idle, inquisitive men and women about our house were very hard to bear: but even this sense of oppression only served to vivify our mutual love. Not only I, but he also, made an effort not to let it be seen that anything in our home was displeasing to us. Sometimes this calmness, this indulgence, this seeming indifference to everything, irritated me, and I could not help looking upon such conduct as weakness, and telling him so.

"Ah, dear Katia," he replied, once, when I was expressing my annoyance, "how can a man show that anything, no matter what, is displeasing to him, when he is as happy as I am? It is a great deal easier to yield, than to make them yield, I have long been convinced of that,—

and, moreover, of the fact there is no situation where one cannot be happy. Everything goes so well with us! I do not even know, any longer, how to get angry; for me, just now, there is nothing at all that is bad, there are only things that are either dull or droll. But, above all, 'let well enough alone.' You may hardly believe me, but whenever I hear a ring at the door-bell, whenever I receive a letter, actually whenever I wake in the morning, a fear takes hold of me, fear of the obligations of life, fear that something may be going to change; for nothing could be better than this present moment!"

I believed him, but I could not understand him. I was happy, but it seemed to me that all was as it ought to be, and could not be otherwise; that it was the same with every one else, and that somewhere there were other joys still, not greater ones, but quite different.

Thus two months passed by, bringing us to the cold, stormy winter, and although he was with me, I began to feel somewhat alone; I began to feel that life was doing nothing but repeating itself, as it were; that it offered nothing new either for me or for him; that, on the contrary, we seemed to be forever treading over and over again in our own footsteps. He was more frequently occupied with business matters away from me, than he had been at first, and once more I had the old feeling that far down in his soul lay a world, hidden and reserved, to which he would not admit me. His unalterable serenity irritated me. I loved him no less than formerly, was no less happy in his love; but my love remained stationary and did not seem to grow any more, and besides this love a new sentiment, full of anxiety, came creeping into my heart. Continuing to love seemed to me so small a thing after that great transport of first loving him; I felt as if my sentiments ought to include agitation, danger, sacrifice of myself. There were in me exuberant forces finding no employment in our tranquil existence, fits of depression which I sought to conceal from him as something wicked, fits of impetuous tenderness and gaiety which only alarmed him. He still had his old habit of watching me and studying my moods, and one day he came to me with a proposal to move to the city for a time; but I begged him not to go, not to alter anything whatever in our mode of life, not to touch our happiness. And, really and truly, I was happy; but I was tormenting myself because this happiness brought me no labor, no sacrifice, while, I felt all the powers of sacrifice and labor dying away within me. I loved him, I knew that I was entirely his; but I wished every one to see our love, wished that some one would try to prevent my loving him,—and then to love him all the same! My mind, and even my sentiments, found their field of action, but yet there was something—the sense of youth, with its need of movement—which had no sufficient satisfaction in our placid life. Why did he tell me that we could go to the city whenever the fancy seized me to do so? If he had not said this, perhaps I might have understood that the feeling which oppressed me was a pernicious chimera, a fault of which I was guilty.... But the thought kept coming into my head that simply by going to the city, I could escape from my ennui; but then, on the other hand, this would be withdrawing him from a life that he loved; I was ashamed to do this, but it cost me something not to do it.

Time went on, the snow piled higher and higher against the walls of the house, and we were always alone, still alone, always with each other, while away yonder,—I knew not where, but yonder somewhere,—in stir and motion, in splendor and excitement, was the crowd, feeling, suffering, rejoicing, amusing itself, without one thought of us and our vanished existence. Worst of all to me was the consciousness that day by day the chain of habit was binding and pressing our life closer into its narrow mould, that our love itself would enter into bondage and become subject to the monotonous and dispassionate law of time. To be cheerful in the morning, respectful at dinner, affectionate in the evening! "To do good!" I said to myself, it is all very well and admirable to do good, and to live a worthy life, as he says; but we have yet time enough for that; there are other things for which, to-day, I feel powers within me. This is not what I wanted; what I wanted was combat, struggle; was to feel that love is our guide in life, not that life guides our love. I could have wished to draw near to the abyss with him, to say to him: "One more step, and I dash myself down, one more movement and I perish;" he, while paling on the brink of this abyss, he would have seized me with his powerful hand, held me there suspended above the gulf, my heart faint with fear,—and then he might have borne me whithersoever he would!

This mood of my soul began to tell upon my health, my nerves began to be out of order. One morning I felt even more upset than usual, and Sergius returned home in rather a bad temper, which was an extremely rare occurrence with him; I noticed it at once, and asked him what was the matter, but he would not tell me, only remarking that it was not worth while. As I afterwards learned, the ispravnik,[G] from ill-will to my

[G] Justice of the peace, of the district.

husband, had summoned several peasants, made some illegal exaction of them, and had even uttered menaces against him. My husband had not yet been able to look into the matter and, moreover, as it was but a piece of absurd impertinence he had not cared to tell me of it; but I imagined that his not telling me was because he considered me a child, and that in his eyes I was incapable of understanding what interested him. I turned from him in silence, without saying a word; he went into his study, gravely, and shut his door after him. When I could no longer hear him, I sat down on a divan, almost crying. "Why," said I to myself, "does he persist in humiliating me by his solemn calmness, by being always in the right? Am I not in the right also, when I am wearied, when everywhere I feel emptiness, when I long to live, to move, not to stay forever in one place and feel time walk over me? I wish to go onward, each day, each hour; I wish for something new, while he,—he wants to stand still in one spot, and keep me standing there with him! And yet how easy it would be for him to satisfy me! He need not take me to the city, it would only be necessary for him to be a little like me, for him to stop trying to constrain and crush himself with his own hands, for him to live naturally. That is what he is always advising me, and it is he who is not natural, that is all."

I felt my tears getting the mastery of me, and my irritation against him increasing. I was afraid of this irritation, and I went to find him. He was sitting in his study, writing. Hearing my steps, he turned for an instant, looked at me with a calm and indifferent air, and continued writing; this look did not please me, and instead of going up to him, I stopped near the table where he was writing and, opening a book, began to run my eyes over the page. He turned then, a second time, and looked at me again:

"Katia, you are not as bright as usual!"

I only responded by a cold glance, meant to convey: "And why? And why so much amiability?" He shook his head at me, and smiled timidly and tenderly; but, for the first time, my smile would not answer his.

"What was the matter with you this morning?" I asked, "why would you tell me nothing?"

"It was a trifle! a slight worry," he replied. "I can tell you all about it, now. Two peasants had been summoned to the city...."

But I would not let him finish.

"Why did you not tell me when I asked you?"

"I might have said something foolish, I was angry then."

"That was just the time to tell me."

"And why so?"

"What you think, then, is that I never can help you in anything?"

"What I think?" said he, throwing down his pen. "I think that without you I could not live. In all things, in all, not only are you a help to me, but it is by you that everything is done. You are literally to me 'well-fallen,'" he went on smiling. "It is in you alone that I live; it seems to me nothing is good but because you are there, because you must...."

"Yes, I know it, I am a nice little child who has to be petted and kept quiet," said I, in such a tone that he looked at me in amazement. "But I do not want this quieting; I have had enough of it!"

"Come, let me tell you about this morning's trouble," he said hastily, as if he was afraid to give me time to say more: "let us see what you think of it!"

"I do not wish to hear it now," I replied.

I really did want to hear it, but it was more agreeable to me, at this moment, to disturb his tranquillity.

"I do not wish to play with the things of life; I wish to live," I added; "like you."

His face, which always so clearly and so readily reflected every impression, wore a look of suffering and intense attention.

"I wish to live with you in perfect equality...."

But I could not finish, such profound pain was on his face. He was silent an instant.

"And in what do you not live with me on a footing of equality?" he said: "it is I, not you, that is concerned in this affair of the ispravnik and some drunken peasants."

"Yes, but it is not only this case," said I.

"For the love of God, do understand me, my darling," he continued; "I know how painful a thing care is for us all; I have lived, and I know it. I love you, therefore I would spare you every care. My life is centred in my love for you; so do not prevent my living!"

"You are always right," said I, without looking at him.

I could not bear to see him once more serene and tranquil, while I was so full of anger and a feeling somewhat resembling repentance.

"Katia! What is the matter with you?" said he. "The question is not in the least which of us two is in the right, what we were talking about is something entirely different! What have you against me? Do not tell me at once; reflect, and then tell me all that is in your thoughts. You are displeased with me, you have, no doubt, a reason, but explain to me in what I am to blame."

But how could I tell him all that I had in the bottom of my heart? The thought that he had seen through me at once, that again I found myself as a child before him, that I could do nothing that he did not comprehend and foresee, excited me more than ever.

"I have nothing against you," said I, "but I am tired, and I do not like ennui. You say that this must be so, and, of course, once more you are right!"

As I spoke, I looked in his face. My object was attained; his serenity had disappeared; alarm and pain were stamped upon his face.

"Katia!" he began, in a low, agitated voice, "this is no jesting we are engaged in, at this moment. Our fate is being decided. I ask you to say nothing, only to hear me. Why are you torturing me thus?"

But I broke in.

"Say no more, you are right," said I, coldly, as if it were not I, but some evil spirit speaking with my lips.

"If you knew what you are doing!" he exclaimed in a trembling voice.

I began to cry, and I felt my heart somewhat relieved. He was sitting near me, silent. I was sorry for him, ashamed of myself, troubled by what I had done. I did not look at him. I felt sure that he was looking at me, and that his eyes were perplexed or severe. I turned; his eyes were indeed fixed upon me, but they were kind and gentle and seemed entreating forgiveness. I took his hand, and said:

"Pardon me! I do not know, myself, what I said."

"Yes, but I know what you said, and I know that you spoke the truth."

"What truth?" I asked.

"That we must go to St. Petersburg. This is no longer the place for us."

"As you wish."

He took me in his arms and kissed me.

"You forgive me?" he said, "I have been to blame concerning you...."

In the evening I was at the piano a long time playing for him, while he walked up and down the room, repeating something in a low tone to himself. This was a habit with him, and I often asked him what he was murmuring thus, and he, still thoughtful, would repeat it again to me; generally it was poetry, sometimes some really absurd thing, but even the very absurdity would show me what frame of mind he was in.

"What are you murmuring there, now?" I asked after a time.

He stood still, thought a little, then, smiling, repeated the two lines from Lermontoff:

> "And he, the madman, invoked the tempest,
> As if, in the tempest, peace might reign!"

"Yes, he is more than a man; he sees everything!" thought I; "how can I help loving him!"

I left the piano, took hold of his hand, and began to walk up and down with him, measuring my steps by his.

"Well!" he said, looking down at me with a smile.

"Well!" I echoed; and our two hearts seemed to spring to each other once more.

At the end of a fortnight, before the fêtes, we were in St. Petersburg.

CHAPTER-VII

OUR removal to St. Petersburg, a week in Moscow, visits to his relatives and to my own, settling ourselves in our new apartment, the journey, the new city, the new faces, all seemed to me like a dream. All was so novel, so changeful, so gay, all was so brightened for me by his presence, by his love, that the placid country life appeared to me something very far off, a sort of unreal thing. To my great surprise, instead of the arrogant pride, the coldness, I had expected to encounter, I was welcomed by all (not only by our relatives, but by strangers,) with such cordiality that it seemed as if they had no thought of anything but me, and as if one and all had been longing for my arrival to complete their own happiness. Contrary to my anticipations, in the circles of society, even in those which seemed to me most select, I discovered many friends and connections of my husband whom he had never mentioned to me, and it often struck me as strange and disagreeable to hear him utter severe strictures upon some of these persons who seemed to me so good. I could not understand why he treated them so coldly, or why he tried to avoid some acquaintances whose intimacy I thought rather flattering. I thought that the more one knew of nice people, the better it was, and all these were nice people.

"Let us see how we shall arrange things," he had said to me before we left the country: "here, we are little Croesuses, and there we shall be far from rich; so we cannot remain in the city longer than Easter, and we cannot go much into society, or we shall find ourselves embarrassed; and I would not like you...."

"Why go into society?" I had answered; "we will only visit our relatives, go to the theatre and opera, and to hear any good music, and even before Easter we can be at home again in the country."

But scarcely were we in St. Petersburg than all these fine plans were forgotten. I had been suddenly thrown into a world so new, so happy, so many delights had surrounded me, so many objects of heretofore unknown interest were offered to me, that all in a moment, as it were, and without being conscious of it, I disavowed all my past, I upset all the plans formerly arranged. Until now there had been nothing but play; as to life itself, it had not yet begun; but here it was now, the real, the true,—and what will it be in the future? thought I. The anxieties, the fits of depression, which came upon me in the country, disappeared suddenly as if by enchantment. My love for my husband became calmer, and, on the other hand, it never occurred to me, in this new life, to think that he was loving me less than formerly. Indeed, it was not possible for me to doubt this love; each thought was instantly understood by him, each sentiment shared, each wish gratified. His unalterable serenity had vanished, here, or perhaps it had only ceased to cause me any irritation. I even felt that besides his old love for me he seemed now to find some new charm in me. Often, after a visit, after I had made some new acquaintance, or after an evening at home, when, with secret misgiving lest I should commit some blunder, I had been performing the duties of hostess, he would say to me:

"Well, my little girl! bravo! well done, indeed!"

This would fill me with delight.

A short time after our arrival he wrote to his mother, and, as he handed me the letter to let me add a few words, he said I must not read what he had written; I laughingly persisted in seeing it, and read:

"You would not recognize Katia, I hardly recognize her myself. Where could she have acquired this lovely and graceful ease of manner, this affability, this fascination, this sweet, unconscious tact? And still always so simple, so gentle, so full of kindness. Every one is delighted with her; and as for me, I am never tired of admiring her, and, if that were possible, would be more in love with her than ever."

"This, then, is what I am?" I thought. And it gave me so much pleasure and gratification that I felt as if I loved him more than ever. My success with all our acquaintances was a thing absolutely unexpected by me. On all sides I was told: here, that I had particularly pleased my uncle, there, that an aunt was raving over me; by this one, that there was not a woman in all St. Petersburg like me; by that one, that if I chose there would not be a woman in society so sought after as myself. There was one cousin of my husband especially, Princess D., a lady of high rank and fashion, no longer young, who announced that she had fallen in love with me at first sight, and who did more than any one else to turn my head with flattering attentions. When, for the first time, this cousin proposed to me to go to a ball, and broached the subject to my husband, he turned towards me with an almost imperceptible smile, and mischievous glance, and asked if I wanted to go. I nodded, and felt my face flush.

"One would say, a little culprit, confessing a wish," he said, laughing good-humoredly.

"You told me we must not go into company, and that you would not like it," I responded, smiling also, and giving him an entreating glance.

"If you wish it very much, we will go."

"Indeed, I would rather...."

"Do you wish it, wish it very much?" he repeated.

I made no answer.

"The greatest harm is not in the world, society, itself," he went on; "it is unsatisfied worldly aspirations that are so evil, so unhealthful. Certainly we must go,—and we will go," he concluded, unhesitatingly.

"To tell you the truth," I replied, "there is nothing in the world I long for so much as to go to this ball!"

We went to it, and my delight was far beyond all my anticipations. At this ball, even more than before, it seemed to me that I was the centre around which everything was revolving; that it was for me alone that this splendid room was in a blaze of light, that the music was sounding, that the gay throng was gathering in ecstasy before me. All, from the hair-dresser and my maid to the dancers, and even the stately old gentlemen who slowly walked about through the rooms, watching the younger people, seemed to me to be either implying or telling me in downright speech that they were wild about me. The impression which I produced at this ball, and which my cousin proudly confided to me, was summed up in the general verdict that I was not the least in the world like other women, and that there was about me some peculiar quality which recalled the simplicity and charm of the country. This success flattered me so much that I frankly owned to my husband how I longed to go to at least two or three of the balls to be given in the course of the winter, "in order," I said, despite a sharp little whisper from my conscience, "that I may be satiated, once for all!"

My husband willingly consented to this, and at first accompanied me, with evident pride and pleasure in my success, apparently forgetting or disavowing what he had formerly decided on principle.

But after awhile I could see that he was bored, and growing tired of the life we were leading. However, this was not yet clear enough to my eyes for me to understand the full significance of the grave, watchful look he sometimes directed towards me, even if I noticed the look at all. I was so intoxicated by this love which I seemed so suddenly to have aroused in all these strangers, by this perfume of elegance, pleasure, and novelty, which I here breathed for the first time; by the apparent removal of what had hitherto, as it were, held me down, namely, the moral weight of my husband; it was so sweet to me, not only to walk through this new world on a level with him, but to find the place given me there even higher than his, and yet to love him with all the more strength and independence than before; that I could not understand that he looked on with displeasure at my utter delight in this worldly existence.

I felt a new thrill of pride and deep satisfaction, when upon entering a ball-room, all eyes would turn towards me; and when he, as if disdaining to parade before the multitude his rights of proprietorship, would quietly and at once leave my side and go off to be lost in the mass of black coats.

"Only wait!" I often thought, as my eyes sought him out at the end of the room, and rested on his face, dimly seen from the distance between us, but sometimes with a very weary look upon it; "wait! when we are at home again you shall see and know for whom I have been glad to be so beautiful and so brilliant, you shall know whom I love far, far above all around me this evening." It seemed to me, very sincerely, that my delight in my successes was only for his sake, and also because they enabled me to sacrifice even themselves for him. "One thing alone," I thought, "might be a danger to me in this life in the world: that is, that one of the men I meet here might conceive a passion for me, and my husband might grow jealous of him; but he had such confidence in me, he appeared to be so calm and indifferent, and all these young men seemed in my eyes so empty in comparison with him, that this peril, the only one, as I thought, with which social life could threaten me, had no terrors at all. Still, the attentions I received from so many persons in society gave me such pleasure, such a sense of satisfied self-love that I rather felt as if there was some merit in my very love for my husband, while at the same time it seemed to impress upon my relation to him greater ease and freedom.

"I noticed how very animated your manner was, while you were talking to N. N.," I said to him, one evening, upon our return from a ball; and I shook my finger at him as I named a well-known lady of St. Petersburg with whom he had spent part of the evening. I only meant to tease him a little, for he was silent, and had a wearied look.

"Ah, why say such a thing? And for you to say it, Katia!" he exclaimed, frowning, and pressing his lips together as if in physical pain. "That is not like you,—not becoming your position, or mine. Leave such speeches to others; bad jests of that kind might entirely do away with our good understanding,—and I still hope that this good understanding may return."

I felt confused, and was silent.

"Will it return, Katia? What do you think?" he asked.

"It is not changed,—it will never change," I said, and then I firmly believed my assertion.

"May God grant it!" he exclaimed, "but it is time we were going back to the country."

This was the only occasion upon which he spoke to me in this way, and the rest of the time it seemed to me that everything was going on as delightfully for him as for me,—and as for me, oh! I was so light-hearted, so joyous! If occasionally I happened to notice that he was wearied, I would console myself by reflecting how long, for his sake, I had been wearied in the country; if our relations seemed to be undergoing some little alteration, I thought how speedily they would resume their old charm when we should find ourselves again alone, in the summer, at our own Nikolski.

Thus the winter sped away without my realizing it; and Easter came, and, despite all our resolutions we were still in St. Petersburg.

The Sunday following, however, we were really ready to go, everything was packed, my husband had made his final purchases of flowers, gifts, things of all kinds which were needed for the country, and was in one of his happiest, most affectionate moods. Shortly before we were to start, we had an unexpected visit from our cousin, who came to beg us to postpone our departure one week, so that we might attend a reception given by Countess R. on Saturday. She reminded me that I had already received several invitations from Countess R., which had been declined, and told me that Prince M., then in St. Petersburg, had, at the last ball, expressed a desire to make my acquaintance, that it was with this object in view that he purposed attending this reception, and that he was saying everywhere that I was the loveliest woman in Russia. The whole city would be there,—in one word, I must go! It would be nothing without me.

My husband was at the other end of the room, talking to some one.

"So you will certainly come, Katia?" said my cousin.

"We meant to leave for the country, day after to-morrow," I replied, doubtfully, as I glanced at my husband. Our eyes met, and he turned away abruptly.

"I will persuade him to stay," said my cousin, "and on Saturday we will turn all heads,—won't we?"

"Our plans would be disarranged, all our packing is done," I objected feebly, beginning to waver.

"Perhaps she had better go to-day, at once, to pay her respects to the prince!" observed my husband from his end of the room, with some irritation, and in a dictatorial tone I had never heard from him before.

"Why, he is getting jealous; I see it for the first time!" exclaimed our cousin, ironically. "It is not for the prince alone, Sergius Mikaïlovitch, but for all of us, that I want her. That is why Countess R. is so urgent."

"It depends upon herself," returned my husband, coldly, as he left the room.

I had seen that he was much more agitated than usual; this troubled me, and I would not give a decided answer to my cousin. As soon as she was gone, I went to look for my husband. He was thoughtfully walking up and down his chamber, and neither saw nor heard me, as I stole softly in on tiptoe.

"He is picturing to himself his dear Nikolski," thought I, watching him, "he is thinking about his morning coffee in that light drawing-room, his fields, his peasants, his evenings at home, and his secret little night suppers! Yes," I decided, in my own mind, "I would give all the balls in the world, and the flatteries of every prince in the universe, to have again his bright joyousness and his loving caresses!"

I was about telling him that I was not going to the reception, that I no longer cared to go, when he suddenly glanced behind him. At the sight of me, his brow darkened, and the dreamy gentleness of his countenance changed entirely. The well-known look came to his face, the look of penetrating wisdom and patronizing calmness. He would not let me see in him simple human nature: he must remain for me the demi-god upon his pedestal!

"What is it, my love?" he enquired, turning towards me with quiet carelessness.

I did not answer. I resented his hiding himself from me, his not allowing me to see him as I best loved him.

"So you wish to go to this reception, on Saturday?" he continued.

"I did wish to go," I replied, "but it did not suit you. And then, too, the packing is done," I added.

Never had he looked at me so coldly, never spoken so coldly.

"I shall not leave before Tuesday, and I will order the packing to be undone," he said; "we will not go until you choose. Do me the favor to go to this entertainment. I shall not leave the city."

As was his habit when excited, he went on walking about the room with quick, irregular steps, and did not look at me.

"Most decidedly, I do not understand you," I said, putting myself in his way, and following him with my eyes. "Why do you speak to me in such a singular manner? I am quite ready to sacrifice this pleasure to you, and you, with sarcasm you have never before shown, you require that I shall go!"

"Come! come! You *sacrifice* yourself" (he laid strong emphasis on the word), "and I, I *sacrifice* myself also! Combat of generosity! There, I hope, is what may be called 'family happiness'!"

This was the first time I had ever heard from his lips words so hard and satirical. His satire did not touch, and his hardness did not frighten me, but they became contagious. Was it really he, always so opposed to any debating between us, always so simple and straightforward, who was speaking to me thus? And why? Just because I had offered to sacrifice myself to his pleasure, which was really the supreme thing in my eyes; just because, at this moment, with the thought, came the comprehension of how much I loved him. Our characters were reversed; it was he who had lost all frankness and simplicity, and I who had found them.

"You are so changed," said I, sighing. "Of what am I guilty in your eyes? It is not this reception, but some old sin, which you are casting up against me in your heart. Why not use more sincerity? You were not afraid of it with me, once. Speak out,—what have you against me?"

"No matter what he may say," I thought, quickly running over the events of the season in my mind, "there is not one thing that he has a right to reproach me with, this whole winter."

I went and stood in the middle of the room, so that he would be obliged to pass near me, and I looked at him. I said to myself: "He will come close to me, he will put his arms around me and kiss me, and that will be the end of it all;" this thought darted into my head, and it even cost me something to let it end so, without my proving to him that he was in the wrong. But he stood still at the end of the room, and, looking in my face:

"You still do not understand me?" he said.

"No."

"Yet ... how can I tell you?... I am appalled, for the first time, I am appalled at what I see—what I cannot but see." He stopped, evidently frightened at the rough tone of his voice.

"What do you mean?" I demanded, indignant tears filling my eyes.

"I am appalled that, knowing the prince's comments on your beauty, you should, after that, be so ready and willing to run after him, forgetting your husband, yourself, your own dignity as a woman,—and then for you not to understand what your husband has to feel in your stead, since you yourself have not this sense of your own dignity!—far from it, you come and declare to your husband that you will *sacrifice* yourself, which is equivalent to saying, 'To please His Highness would be my greatest happiness, but I will *sacrifice* it.'"

The more he said, the more the sound of his own voice excited him, and the harder, more cutting and violent, became his voice. I had never seen, and had never expected to see him thus; the blood surged to my heart; I was frightened, but yet, at the same time, a sense of unmerited disgrace and offended self-love aroused me, and I keenly longed to take some vengeance on him.

"I have long expected this outbreak," said I, "speak, speak!"

"I do not know what you may have expected," he went on, "but I might have anticipated still worse things, from seeing you day by day steeped in this slime, this idleness, this luxury, this senseless society; and I did anticipate.... I did anticipate this that to-day covers me with shame, and sinks me in misery such as I have never experienced; shame for myself, when your dear friend, prying and fumbling about in my heart with her unclean fingers, spoke of my jealousy,—and jealousy of whom? Of a man whom neither you nor I have ever seen! And you, as if purposely, you will not understand me, you 'will sacrifice' to me,—whom? Great God!... Shame on your degradation! Sacrifice!" he repeated once more.

"Ah, this then is what is meant by the husband's authority," I thought. "To insult and humiliate his wife, who is not guilty of the very least thing in the world! Here then are 'marital rights;'—but I, for one, will never submit to them!"

"Well, I sacrifice *nothing* to you, then," I returned, feeling my nostrils dilate, and my face grow bloodless. "I will go to the reception on Saturday. I most certainly will go!"

"And God give you pleasure in it! Only—all is ended between us!" he exclaimed, in an uncontrollable transport of rage. "At least you shall not make a martyr of me any longer. I was a fool who...."

But his lips trembled, and he made a visible effort not to finish what he had begun to say.

At this moment I was afraid of him and I hated him. I longed to say a great many more things to him, and to avenge myself for all his insults; but if I had so much as opened my lips, my tears could no longer have been restrained, and I would have felt my dignity compromised before him. I left the room, without a word. But scarcely was I beyond the sound of his footsteps when I was suddenly seized with terror at the thought of what we had done. It seemed to me horrible that, perhaps for life, this bond, which constituted all my happiness, was destroyed, and my impulse was to return at once. But would his passion have subsided sufficiently for him to comprehend me, if, without a word, I should hold out my hand to him, and look into his eyes? Would he comprehend my generosity? Suppose he should regard my sincere sorrow as dissimulation? Or should consider my voluntary right-doing as repentance, and receive me on that score? Or grant me pardon, with proud tranquillity? And why, when I have loved him so much, oh, *why* should he have insulted me so?

I did not go back to him, but into my own room, where I sat for a long time, crying, recalling with terror every word of our conversation, mentally substituting other words for those we had used, adding different and better ones, then reminding myself again, with a mingled sense of fright and outraged feeling, of all that had taken place. When I came down to tea, in the evening, and in the presence of C., who was making us a visit, met my husband again, I was aware that from this day forward there must be an open gulf between us. C. asked me when we were going to leave the city. I could not answer her.

"On Tuesday," replied my husband, "we are staying for Countess R's reception. You are going, no doubt?" he continued, turning to me.

I was frightened at the sound of his voice, although it seemed quite as usual, and glanced at my husband. His eyes were fixed on me, with a hard ironical look, his tone was measured, cold.

"Yes," I replied.

Later, when we were alone, he approached me, and holding out his hand:

"Forget, I entreat you, what I said to you."

I took his hand, a faint smile came to my trembling lips, and the tears started to my eyes; but he quickly drew it away and, as if fearing a sentimental scene, went and sat down in an arm-chair at some distance from me. "Is it possible that he still believes himself right?" thought I; and I had on my lips a cordial explanation, and a request not to go to the reception.

"I must write to mamma that we have postponed our departure," said he, "or she will be uneasy."

"And when do you intend to leave?" I asked.

"On the Tuesday after the reception."

"I hope this is not on my account," said I, looking into his eyes, but they only looked back into mine without telling me anything, as if they were held far from me by some secret force. All at once, his face appeared to me old and disagreeable.

We went to the reception, and seemingly our relations were again cordial and affectionate, but in reality they were quite unlike what they had been in the past.

At the reception I was sitting in the midst of a circle of ladies, when the prince approached me, so that I was obliged to stand up and speak to him. As I did so, my eyes involuntarily sought my husband; I saw him look at me, from the other end of the room, and then turn away. Such a rush of shame and sorrow came over me, that I felt almost ill, and I knew that my face and neck grew scarlet under the eyes of the prince. But I had to stand and listen to what he was saying to me, all the while feeling him scrutinize me keenly from head to foot. Our conversation was not long, there was not room near me for him to sit down, and he could not help seeing how ill at ease I was with him. We talked of the last ball, where I was to spend the summer, *etc*. Upon leaving me he expressed a wish to make my husband's acquaintance, and in a little while I saw them meet, at the other end of the room, and begin to talk with each other. The prince must have made some remark concerning me, for I saw him smile and glance in my direction.

My husband's face flushed darkly, he bowed, and was the first to conclude the interview. I felt my color rise, also, for I was mortified to think what opinion the prince must have formed of me, and more especially of Sergius. It seemed to me that every one must have observed my embarrassment while I was talking with the prince, and also his very singular manner; "God knows," said I to myself, "what interpretation may be put upon it; could any one happen to know of my wrangle with my husband?" My cousin took me home, and on the way we were talking about him. I could not resist telling her all that had passed between us in regard to this unfortunate reception. She soothed me by assurances that it was only one of those frequent quarrels, which signify nothing at all and leave no result behind them; and in explaining my husband's character from her point of view, she spoke of him as extremely reserved and proud. I agreed with her, and it seemed to me that, after this, I comprehended his character more clearly and much more calmly.

But afterwards, when we were again alone together, this judgment of mine with regard to him appeared to me a real crime, which weighed upon my conscience, and I felt that the gulf between us was widening more and more.

From this day on, our life and our mutual relations suffered a complete change. Being alone together was no longer a delight to us. There were subjects to be avoided, and it was easier for us to talk to each other in the presence of a third person. If in the course of conversation any allusion chanced to be made, either to life in the country, or to balls, dazzling wild-fire seemed to dance before our eyes and make us afraid to look at each other; I knew that his embarrassment was as great as my own; we both realized how far asunder we were thrust by that dividing gulf, and dreaded drawing nearer. I was persuaded that he was passionate and proud, and that I must be very careful not to run against his weak points. And, on his part, he was convinced that I could not exist outside of the life of the world, that a home in the country did not suit me at all, and that he must resign himself to this unhappy predilection. Therefore we both shunned any direct conversation upon such subjects, and each erroneously judged the other. We had long ceased to be respectively, in each other's eyes, the most perfect beings in this world; on the contrary, we were beginning to compare each other with those around us, and to measure with secret appreciation our own characters.

CHAPTER-VIII

I HAD been very unwell before we left St. Petersburg, and instead of going home we moved into a villa at a short distance from the city, where my husband left me while he went to see his mother. I was then quite well enough to accompany him, but he urged me not to do so, alleging as his reason my state of health. I quite understood that he was not really afraid of my health, but he was possessed by the idea that it would not be good for us to be in the country; I did not insist very strenuously, and remained where I was. Without him I felt myself truly in the midst of emptiness and isolation; but when he returned I perceived that his presence no longer added to my life what it had been wont to add. Those former relations, when any thought, any sensation, not communicated to him, oppressed me like a crime; when all his actions, all his words, appeared to me models of perfection; when, from sheer joy, we would laugh at nothing, looking at each other; those relations had so insensibly changed into something quite different, that we ourselves hardly admitted the transformation. But the fact was that each of us had now separate occupations and interests, which we no longer sought to share. We had even ceased to be at all troubled at thus living in entirely distinct worlds, and entirely as strangers to each other. We had become habituated to this thought, and at the end of a year there was no longer the mutual embarrassment when our eyes chanced to meet. His boyishness, his outbursts of light-hearted gaiety when with me, were gone; gone, too, was that indulgent indifference, against which I had so often risen in rebellion; nor had the penetrating look survived, which, in other days, had at once disturbed and delighted me; there were no more of the prayers, no more of the hours of exaltation which we had so loved to share, and indeed we saw each other only very rarely; he was constantly out, and I no longer dreaded remaining alone, no longer complained of it; I was perpetually engrossed, on my side, with the obligations of society, and never felt any need of him whatever.

Scenes and altercations between us were quite unheard-of. I endeavored to satisfy him, he carried out all my wishes, any one would have said that we still loved each other.

When we were alone together, which was of rare occurrence, I felt neither joy, agitation, nor embarrassment, in his presence, any more than if I had been alone. I knew well that here was no new-comer, no stranger, but on the contrary, a very excellent man, in short my husband, whom I knew just as well as I knew myself. I was persuaded that I could tell beforehand all that he would do, all that he would think, precisely what view he would take of any matter, and if he did or thought otherwise I only considered that he made a mistake; I never expected anything at all from him. In one word, it was my husband, that was all. It seemed to me that things were so, and had to be so; that no other relations between us could exist, or indeed ever had existed. When he went away, especially at first, I still felt terribly lonely, and while he was absent I felt the full value of his support; when he came home, I would even throw myself in his arms with joy; but scarcely had two hours elapsed ere I had forgotten this joy, and would find that I had nothing to say to him. In these brief moments, when calm, temperate tenderness seemed to revive between us, it seemed to me that there never had been anything but this; that this alone was what had once so powerfully stirred my heart, and I thought I read in his eyes the same impression. I felt that to this tenderness there was a limit, which he did not wish to pass, and neither did I. Sometimes this caused me a little regret, but I had no time to think about it seriously, and I tried to put it out of my mind, by giving myself up to a variety of amusements of which I did not even render a clear account to myself, but which perpetually offered themselves to me. The life in the world, which, at first, had bewildered me with its splendor and the gratification it afforded to my self-love, had soon established entire dominion over my inclinations, and become at once a habit and a bondage, occupying in my soul that place which I had fancied would be the home of sentiment. Therefore I avoided being alone, dreading lest it might force me to look into and realize my condition. My whole time, from the earliest hour in the morning till the latest at night, was appropriated to something; even if I did not go out, there was no time that I left free. I found in this life neither pleasure, nor weariness, and it seemed to me it had always been thus.

In this manner three years passed away, and our relations with each other remained the same, benumbed, congealed, motionless, as if no alteration could come to them, either for better or worse. During the course of these three years there were two important events in the family, but neither brought any change to my own life. These events were the birth of my first child, and the death of Tatiana Semenovna. At first the maternal sentiment took possession of me with such power, so great and unexpected a rapture seized upon me, that I imagined a new existence was beginning; but at the end of two months, when I commenced to go into society once more, this sentiment, which had been gradually subsiding, had become nothing more than the habitual and cold performance of a duty. My husband, on the contrary, from the day of this son's birth, had become his old self, gentle, calm, and home-loving, recalling for his child, all his former tenderness and gaiety. Often when I went in my ball-dress into the child's nursery, to give him the evening benediction before starting and found my husband there, I would catch a glance of reproach, or a severe and watchful look fixed upon me, and I would all at once feel ashamed. I was myself terrified at my indifference towards my own child, and I asked myself: "Can I be so much worse than other women?—But what is to be done?" I questioned. "Of course I love my son, but, for all that, I cannot sit down beside him for whole days at a time, that would bore me to death; and as for making a pretence, nothing in the world would induce me to do such a thing!"

The death of my husband's mother was a great grief to him; it was very painful to him, he said, to live after her at Nikolski, but though I also regretted her and really sympathized with his sorrow, it would have been at that time more agreeable, more restful to me, to return and make our residence there. We had passed the greater part of these three years in the city; once only had I been at Nikolski, for a visit of two months; and during the third year we had been abroad.

We passed this summer at the baths.

I was then twenty-one years of age. We were, I thought, prosperous; from my home life I expected no more than it had already given me; all the people whom I knew, it seemed to me, loved me; my health was excellent, I knew that I was pretty, my *toilettes* were the freshest at the baths, the weather was superb, an indefinable atmosphere of beauty and elegance surrounded me, and everything appeared to me in the highest degree delightful and joyous. Yet I was not, as light-hearted as I had been in the old days at Nikolski, when I had felt that my happiness was within myself, when I was happy because I deserved to be so, when my happiness was great but might be greater still. Now all was different;

nevertheless the summer was charming. I had nothing to desire, nothing to hope, nothing to fear; my life, as it seemed to me, was at its full, and my conscience, it also seemed to me, was entirely clear.

Among the men most conspicuous at the baths during this season, there was not one whom, for any reason whatever, I preferred above the others, not even old Prince K. our ambassador, who paid me distinguished attention. One was too young, another was too old, this one was an Englishman with light curly hair, that one, a bearded Frenchman; I was perfectly indifferent to all, but, at the same time, all were indispensable to me. Insignificant as they might be, they yet belonged to, and formed a part of, this life of elegance surrounding me, this atmosphere in which I breathed. However, there was one among them, an Italian, Marquis D. who, by the bold fashion in which he showed the admiration he felt for me, had attracted my attention more than the others. He allowed no occasion to escape him of meeting me, dancing with me, appearing on horseback beside me, accompanying me to the casino, and he was constantly telling me how beautiful I was. From my window I sometimes saw him wandering around our house, and more than once the annoying persistence of the glances shot towards me from his flashing eyes had made me blush and turn away.

He was young, handsome, elegant; and one remarkable thing about him was his extraordinary resemblance to my husband, especially in his smile and something about the upper part of the face, though he was the handsomer man of the two. I was struck by the likeness, in spite of decided differences in some particulars, in the mouth for instance, the look, the longer shape of the chin; and instead of the charm given to my husband's face by his expression of kindness and ideal calmness, there was in the other something gross and almost bestial. After a while I could not help seeing that he was passionately in love with me; I sometimes found myself thinking of him with lofty pity. I undertook to tranquillize him, and bring him down to terms of cordial confidence and friendship, but he repelled these attempts with trenchant disdain, and, to my great discomfiture, continued to show indications of a passion, silent, indeed, as yet, but momentarily threatening to break forth. Although I would not acknowledge it to myself, I was afraid of this man, and seemed, against my own will, as it were, forced to think of him. My husband had made his acquaintance, and was even more intimate with him than with most of our circle, with whom he confined himself to being simply the husband of his wife, and to whom his bearing was haughty and cold.

Towards the end of the season I had a slight illness, which confined me to the house for two weeks. The first time I went out, after my recovery, was to listen to the music in the evening, and I was at once told of the arrival of Lady C. a noted beauty, who had been expected for some time. A circle of friends quickly gathered around me, eagerly welcoming me once more among them, but a yet larger circle was forming about the new belle, and everybody near me was telling me about her and her beauty. She was pointed out to me; a beautiful and bewitching woman, truly, but with an expression of confidence and self-sufficiency which impressed me unpleasantly, and I said so. That evening, everything that usually seemed so bright and delightful was tiresome to me. The following day Lady C. organized an expedition to the castle, which I declined. Hardly any one remained behind with me, and the aspect of affairs was decidedly changed to my eyes. All, men and things, seemed stupid and dull; I felt like crying, and resolved to complete my cure as soon as possible and go home to Russia. At the bottom of my heart lurked bad, malevolent feelings, but I would not confess it to myself. I said that I was not well, making that a pretext for giving up society. I very seldom went out, and then only in the morning, alone, to drink the waters, or for a quiet walk or drive about the environs with L. M., one of my Russian acquaintances. My husband was absent at this time, having gone, some days before, to Heidelberg, to wait there until the end of my prescribed stay should allow our return to Russia, and he came to see me only now and then.

One day Lady C. had carried off most of the company on some party of pleasure, and after dinner L. M. and I made a little excursion to the castle by ourselves. While our carriage was slowly following the winding road between the double rows of chestnuts, centuries old, between whose gray trunks we saw in the distance the exquisite environs of Baden, lying in the purple light of the setting sun, we unconsciously fell into a serious strain of conversation, which had never before been the case with us. L. M., whom I had known so long, now for the first time appeared to me as a lovely intelligent woman, with whom one could discuss any topic whatever, and whose society was full of charm and interest. We talked about family duties and pleasures, children, the vacuous life led in such places as we were now in, our desire to return to Russia, to the country, and we both fell into a grave, gentle mood, which was still upon us when we reached the castle. Within its broken walls all was in deep shadow, cool and still, the summits of the towers were yet in the sunlight, and the least sound of voice or footstep re-echoed among the arches. Through the doorway we saw the beautiful stretch of country surrounding Baden,—beautiful, yet to our Russian eyes, cold and stern.

We sat down to rest, silently watching the sinking sun. Presently we heard voices, they grew more distinct, and I thought I caught my own name. I listened involuntarily, and heard a few words. I recognized the voices; they were those of the Marquis D. and of a Frenchman, his friend, whom I also knew. They were talking about me and Lady C. The Frenchman was comparing one with the other, and analyzing our beauty. He said nothing objectionable, yet I felt the blood rush to my heart as he spoke. He entered into detail as to what he found attractive in both Lady C. and myself. As for me, I was already a mother, while Lady C. was but nineteen years of age; my hair was more beautiful, but Lady C.'s was more gracefully arranged; Lady C. was more the high born dame "while yours," he said, alluding to me, "is one of the little princesses so often sent us by Russia." He concluded by saying that it was very discreet in me not to attempt to contest the field with Lady C., for, if I did, I most assuredly would find Baden my burial-place.

This cut me to the quick.

"Unless she chose to console herself with you!" added the Frenchman with a gay, cruel laugh.

"If she goes, I shall follow," was the coarse reply of the voice with the Italian accent.

"Happy mortal! he can still love!" commented the other, mockingly.

"Love!" the Italian was silent a moment, then went on. "I cannot help loving! Without love there is no life. To make of one's life a romance,—that is the only good. And my romances never break off in the middle; this one, like the others, I will carry out to the end."

"Good luck, my friend!" said the Frenchman.

I heard no more for the speakers seemed to turn the angle of the wall, and their steps receded on the other side. They descended the broken stairs, and in a few moments emerged from a side-door near us, showing much surprise at the sight of us. I felt my cheeks flame when Marquis D. approached me, and was confused and frightened at his offering me his arm upon our leaving the castle. I could not refuse it, and following L. M. who led the way with his friend, we went down towards the carriage. I was indignant at what the Frenchman had said of me, though I could not help secretly admitting that he had done nothing but put into language what I myself had already felt, but the words of the marquis had confounded and revolted me by their grossness. I was tortured by the thought of having heard them, and at the same time I had suddenly lost all fear of him. I was disgusted at feeling him so near me; without looking at him, without answering him, trying, though I still had his arm, to keep so far from him that I could not hear his whispers, I walked on quickly, close behind L. M. and the Frenchman. The marquis was talking about the lovely view, the unexpected delight of meeting me, and I know not what besides, but I did not listen to him. The whole time I was thinking about my husband, my son, Russia; divided feelings of shame and pity took hold of me, and I was possessed by a desire to hurry home, to shut myself up in my solitary room in the *Hôtel de Bade*, where I might be free to reflect upon all that seemed so suddenly to have risen up within my soul. But L. M. was walking rather slowly, the carriage was still some distance away, and it seemed to me that my escort was obstinately slackening our pace, as if he meant to be left alone with me. "That shall not be!" I said to myself, quickening my steps. But he undisguisedly kept me back, holding my arm with a close pressure; at this moment L. M. turned a corner of the road, and we were left alone. I was seized with alarm.

"Excuse me," said I coldly, drawing my arm out of his, but the lace caught on one of his buttons. He stooped towards me to disengage it, and his ungloved fingers rested on my arm. A new sensation—not fright, certainly not pleasure—sent a chill shiver through me. I looked up at him, meaning my glance to express all the cold contempt I felt for him; but instead of this, he seemed to read in it only agitation and alarm. His ardent, humid eyes were fixed passionately upon me, his hands grasped my wrists, his half-open lips were murmuring to me, telling me that he loved me, that I was everything to him, his hold upon me growing stronger and closer with every word. I felt fire in my veins, my vision was obscured, I trembled from head to foot, and the words I tried to utter died away in my throat. Suddenly I felt a kiss upon my cheek; I shivered, and looked into his face again, powerless to speak or stir, expecting and wishing I knew not what.

It was only an instant. But this instant was terrible! In it I saw him as he was, I analyzed his face at a glance: low brow, straight correct nose with swelling nostrils, fine beard and mustache waxed and pointed, cheeks carefully shaven, brown neck. I hated him, I feared him, he was a stranger to me; nevertheless, at this moment, how powerfully the emotion and passion of this detestable man, this stranger, was re-echoing within me!

"I love you!" was the murmur of the voice so like my husband's. My husband and my child,—hurriedly my mind flashed to them, as beings dearly loved, once existent, now gone, lost, done with. But suddenly from around the turn of the road I heard L. M.'s voice calling me. I recovered myself, snatched away my hands without looking at him, and almost flew to rejoin her. Not until we were in the caléche did I glance back at him. He took off his hat, and said something to me—I know not what—smiling. He little knew what inexpressible torture he made me endure at that moment.

Life appeared so miserable, the future so desperate, the past so sombre! L. M. talked to me, but I did not understand one word she was saying. It seemed as though she was only talking to me from compassion, and to hide the contempt she felt. I thought I read this contempt, this insulting compassion in every word, every glance. That kiss was burning into my cheek with cutting shame, and to think of my husband and child was insupportable to me. Once alone in my chamber, I hoped to be able to meditate upon my situation, but I found it was frightful to remain alone. I could not drink the tea that was brought me, and without knowing why, hurriedly I decided to take the evening train for Heidelberg, to rejoin my husband. When I was seated with my maid in the empty compartment, when the train was at last in motion, and I breathed the fresh air rushing in through the empty windows, I began to be myself again, and to think with some degree of clearness over my past and my future. All my married life, from the day of our departure for St. Petersburg, lay before me in a new light, that of awakened and accusing conscience.

For the first time, I vividly recalled the commencement of my life in the country, my plans; for the first time, the thought came to my mind: how happy he was then! And I suddenly felt guilty towards him. "But then, why not check me, why dissimulate before me, why avoid all explanation, why insult me?" I asked myself. "Why not use the power of his love? But perhaps he no longer loved me?"—Yet, whether he was to blame or not, here was this on my cheek, this kiss which I still felt.

The nearer I came to Heidelberg, and the more clearly my husband's image presented itself, the more terrible became the imminent meeting with him. "I will tell him all, all; my eyes will be blinded with tears of repentance," thought I, "and he will forgive me." But I did not myself know what was this "all" that I was going to tell him, nor was I absolutely sure that he would forgive me. In fact, when I entered his room and saw his face, so tranquil despite its surprise, I felt no longer able to tell him anything, to confess anything, to entreat his forgiveness for anything. An unspeakable sorrow and deep repentance were weighing me down.

"What were you thinking of?" he said: "I intended joining you at Baden to-morrow." But a second glance at me seemed to startle him. "Is anything wrong? What is the matter with you?" he exclaimed.

"Nothing," I replied, keeping back my tears. "I have come away ... I am not going back ... Let us go—to-morrow if we can—home to Russia!"

He was silent for some time, watching me narrowly.

"Come, tell me what has occurred," he said, at length.

I felt my face grow scarlet, and my eyes sank. His were glittering with an indefinable foreboding, and hot anger. I dreaded the thoughts which might be assailing him, and, with a power of dissimulation of which I could not have believed myself capable, I made haste to answer:

"Nothing has occurred,—but I was overwhelmed by weariness and dejection; I was alone, I began to think of you, and of our life. How long I have been to blame towards you! After this, you may take me with you wherever you wish! Yes, I have long been to blame," I repeated, and my tears began to fall fast. "Let us go back to the country," I cried, "and forever!"

"Ah! my love, spare me these sentimental scenes," said he, coldly; "for you to go to the country will be all very well, just now, for we are running a little short of money; but as for its being 'forever,' that is but a notion: I know you could not stay there long! Come, drink a cup of tea,—that is the best thing to do," he concluded, rising to call a servant.

I could not help imagining what his thoughts of me doubtless were, and I felt indignant at the frightful ideas which I attributed to him as I met the look of shame and vigilant suspicion which he bent upon me. No, he will not, and he cannot comprehend me!... I told him that I was going to see the child, and left him. I longed to be alone, and free to weep, weep, weep....

CHAPTER-IX

OUR house at Nikolski, so long cold and deserted, came to life again; but the thing which did not come to life was our old existence. Mamma was there no longer, and henceforth we were alone, we two alone with each other. But not only was solitude no longer to us what it had once been, but we found it a burden and constraint. The winter passed all the more drearily for me from my being out of health, and it was not until some time after the birth of my second son that I recovered my strength.

My relations with my husband continued cold and friendly, as at St. Petersburg; but here in the country there was not a floor, not a wall, not a piece of furniture, which did not remind me of what he had been to me, and what I had lost. There stood between us, as it were, an offence not forgiven; one would have said that he wished to punish me for something, and that he was pretending to himself to be unconscious of it. How could I ask forgiveness without knowing for what fault? He only punished me by no longer entirely giving himself up to me, by no longer surrendering to me his whole soul; but to no one, and under no circumstances, was his soul surrendered, any more than if he had none. It sometimes came into my head that he was only making a pretence of being what he now was, in order to torment me, and that his feelings were in reality what they had formerly been, and I tried to provoke him into letting this be seen; but he invariably eluded all frank explanation; one would have said that he suspected me of dissimulation, and dreaded all manifestations of tenderness as attempts to ridicule him. His looks and his air seemed to say: "I know all, there is nothing to tell me; all that you would confide to me, I already know; I know that you talk in one manner and act in another." At first I was hurt by his apparent fear of being frank with me, but I soon accustomed myself to the thought that in him this was not so much lack of frankness, as lack of necessity for frankness.

And on my side, my tongue was no longer capable of telling him impulsively, as in the old days, that I loved him, of asking him to read the prayers with me, of calling him to listen to my music when I was going to play; there seemed to be certain rules of formality tacitly decreed between us. We lived our own lives; he, with his various interests and occupations, in which I no longer claimed nor desired a share; I, with my idle hours, about which he no longer seemed to trouble himself. As for the children, they were still too young to be in any way a bond between us.

Spring came. Macha and Sonia returned to the country for the summer; and as Nikolski was undergoing repairs, we went with them to Pokrovski. The same old home, the terrace, the out-of-door tea-table, the piano in the half-lighted room, my own old chamber with its white curtains, and the girlish dreams which seemed to have been left behind there, forgotten. In this chamber were two beds; over one, which had been my own, I now bent nightly to bless my sturdy Kokocha,[H] in the midst of his bedtime frolics; in the other lay little Vasica,[I] his baby-face rosy with sleep, under the soft white blankets. After giving the benediction, I often lingered a long time in this peaceful chamber, and from every corner of its walls, from every fold of its curtains, came stealing around me forgotten visions of my youth; childish songs, gay choruses, floated again to my ears. And what were they now,—these visions? Were they sounding still, anywhere,—these glad and sweet old songs? All that I had hardly dared to hope had come true. My vague and confused dreams had become reality, and it was now my life, so hard, so heavy, so stripped of joy. And yet here around me were not all things as before? Was it not the same garden that I saw beneath my window, the same terrace, the same paths and benches? Far off there, across the ravine, the songs of the nightingales still seemed to rise out of the ripples of the little pond, the lilacs bloomed as they used to do, the moon still stood in white glory over the corner of the house, yet for me all was so changed, so changed! Macha and I had our old quiet talks, sitting together as of old in the salon, and we still talked of him. But Macha's brow was grave, her face was wan, her eyes no longer shone with contentment and hope, but were full of sad sympathy, and almost expressed compassion. We no longer went into ecstasies over him, as

[H] Diminutive of Nicolas.

[I] Yvan.

in the past; we judged him, now; we no longer marvelled at our great happiness and wondered how it came to be ours, we no longer had the impulse to tell all the world what we felt; we whispered in each other's ear like conspirators; for the hundredth time we asked each other why all was so sad, so changed. As for him, he was still the same, except that the line between his brows was deeper, and his temples were more silvery, and his eyes, watchful, deep, continually turned away from me, were darkened by a shadow. I, too, was still the same, but I no longer felt either love or desire to love. No more wish to work, no more satisfaction with myself. And how far off, how impossible, now appeared my old religious fervor, my old love for him, my old fulness of life! I could not, now, even comprehend what in those days was so luminous and so true: the happiness of living for others. Why for others? when I no longer wished to live for myself....

I had entirely given up my music during our residence in St. Petersburg, but now my old piano and my old pieces brought back the love for it.

One day when I was not feeling well, I stayed at home, alone, while Macha and Sonia went with my husband to see the improvements at Nikolski. The tea-table was set, I went down-stairs, and, while waiting for them, seated myself at the piano. I opened the sonata *Quasi una fantasia*, and began to play. No living creature was to be seen or heard, the windows were open upon the garden; the familiar notes, so sad and penetrating, resounded through the room. I concluded the first part, and unconsciously, simply from old habit, I looked across to the corner where he used to sit and listen to me. But he was no longer there, a long-unmoved chair occupied his old place; from the side of the open window a projecting branch of lilac stood out against the burning west, the evening air stole quietly in. I leaned my elbows on the piano, covered my face with both hands, and fell into a fit of musing. I remained there a long time, mournfully recalling the old days, irrevocably gone, and timidly looking at the days to come. But hereafter, it seemed to me, there could be nothing, I could hope nothing, desire nothing. "Is it possible that I have outlived all that!" thought I, raising my head with horror, and in order to forget and to cease thinking, I began to play again, and still the same old *andante*. "My God!" I said, "pardon me if I am guilty, or give back to my soul what made its beauty ... or teach me what I ought to do,—how I ought to live!"

The sound of wheels echoed on the turf and before the door, then I heard on the terrace steady steps, well-known to me, then all was quiet. But it was no longer the old feeling which stirred in me at these familiar footsteps. They came up behind me when I had finished the sonata, and a hand was laid upon my shoulder.

"A happy thought, to play the old sonata!" he said.

I made no answer.

"Have not you had tea?"

I shook my head, without turning towards him, for I did not want him to see the traces of agitation on my face.

"They will be here presently; the horses were a little unruly, and they are coming home on foot, by the road," he continued.

"We will wait for them," I said, going out on the terrace, in the hope that he would follow, but he inquired for the children, and went up to see them. Once more, his presence, the sound of his voice, so kind, so honest, dissuaded me from believing that all was lost for me. "What more is there to desire?" I thought: "he is good and true, he is an excellent husband, an excellent father, and I do not myself know what is missing,—what I want."

I went out on the balcony, and sat down under the awning of the terrace, on the same bench where I was sitting upon the day of our decisive explanation long ago. The sun was nearly down, dusk was gathering; a shade of spring softened the pure sky, where one tiny spark was already gleaming. The light wind had died away, not a leaf or blade of grass stirred; the perfume of the lilacs and cherry-trees, so powerful that one might have thought all the air itself was in bloom, came in puffs over garden and terrace, now faint and now full, making one feel an impulse to close the eyes, to shut out all sight and sound, to banish every sensation save that of inhaling this exquisite fragrance. The dahlias and rose-bushes, yet leafless, stood in still lines in the newly-dug black mould of their beds, lifting their heads above their white props. From afar came the intermittent notes of the nightingales, or the rush of their restless flight from place to place.

It was in vain that I strove to calm myself, I seemed to be waiting and wishing for something.

Sergius came from up-stairs, and sat down beside me.

"I believe it is going to rain," he said, "they will get wet."

"Yes," I replied; and we were both silent.

In the meantime, the cloud, without any wind, had crept slowly and stealthily above our heads; nature was yet more perfectly tranquil, sweet, and still: suddenly one drop fell, and, so to speak, rebounded, upon the linen of the awning, another rolled, a growing ball of dust, along the path; then, with a sound like deadened hail, came the heavy dash of rain, gathering force every moment. At once, as if by concert, frogs and nightingales were silent; but the light plash of the fountain was still heard beneath the beating of the rain, and far off in the distance some little bird, no doubt safe and dry under a sheltering bough, chirped in monotonous rhythm his two recurring notes. Sergius rose to go into the house.

"Where are you going?" said I, stopping him. "It is so delightful here!"

"I must send an umbrella and some overshoes."

"It is not necessary, this will be over directly."

He assented, and we remained standing together by the balustrade of the balcony. I put my hand on the wet slippery rail, and leaned forward into the rain, the cool drops falling lightly on my hair and neck. The cloud, brightening and thinning, scattered in shining spray above us, the regular beat of the shower was succeeded by the sound of heavy drops falling more and more rarely from the sky or from the trees. The frogs resumed their croaking, the nightingales shook their wings and began again to respond to each other from behind the glistening shrubs, now on one side, now on another. All was serene again before us.

"How good it is to live!" he said, leaning over the balustrade and passing his hand over my wet hair.

This simple caress acted on me like a reproach, and I longed to let my tears flow.

"What more can a man need?" continued he. "I am at this moment so content, that I feel nothing wanting, and I am completely happy!"

("You did not speak so to me when to hear it would have made my happiness," I thought. "However great yours was, then, you used to say that you wished for more of it, still more. And now you are calm and content, when my soul is full of inexpressible repentance and unsatisfied tears!")

"To me, too, life is good," said I, "and it is precisely because it is so good to me, that I am sad. I feel so detached, so incomplete; I am always wanting some other thing, and yet everything here is so good, so tranquil! Can it be possible that for you no sorrow ever seems mingled with your pleasure in life?—as if, for instance, you were feeling regret for something in the past?"

He drew away the hand resting on my head, and was silent for a moment.

"Yes, that has been the case with me, formerly, particularly in the spring," he said, as if searching his memory. "Yes, I also have spent whole nights in longings and fears,—and what beautiful nights they were!... But then all was before me, and now all is behind; now I am content with what is, and that to me is perfection," he concluded, with such easy frankness of manner, that, painful as it was to hear, I was convinced that it was the truth.

"Then you desire nothing more?" I questioned.

"Nothing impossible," he replied, divining my thought. "How wet you have made your head," he went on, caressing me like a child, and passing his hand again over my hair; "you are jealous of the leaves and grass which the rain was falling on; you would like to be the grass and the leaves and the rain; while I—I enjoy simply seeing them, as I do seeing whatever is good, young, happy."

"And you regret nothing in the past?" I persisted, with the dull weight on my heart growing heavier and heavier.

He seemed to muse for a moment, keeping silent. I saw that he wished to answer honestly.

"No!" he said, at length, briefly.

"That is not true! that is not true!" I cried, turning and facing him, with my eyes fixed upon his. "You do not regret the past?"

"No!" he repeated. "I bless it, but I do not regret it."

"And you would not wish to go back to it?"

He turned away, looking out over the garden.

"I no more wish that than I would wish to have wings. It cannot be."

"And you would not re-make this past? And you reproach neither yourself, nor me?"

"Never! all has been for the best."

"Listen!" said I, seizing his hand to force him to turn towards me. "Listen! Why did you never tell me what you wished from me, that I might have lived exactly as you desired? Why did you give me a liberty which I knew not how to use? why did you cease to teach me? If you had wished it, if you had cared to guide me differently, nothing, nothing would have happened," I went on, in a voice which more and more energetically expressed anger and reproach, with none of the former love.

"What is it that would not have happened?" said he with surprise, turning towards me. "There has been nothing. All is well, very well," he repeated smiling.

"Can it be possible," I thought, that he does not understand me? "or, worse still, that he will not understand me?" and my tears began to fall.

"This would have happened,—that, not having made me guilty towards you, you would not have punished me by your indifference, your contempt," I broke out. "What would *not* have happened is seeing myself, with no fault on my own part, suddenly robbed by you of all that was dear to me."

"What are you saying, my darling?" he exclaimed, as if he had not understood my words.

"No, let me finish! You have robbed me of your confidence, your love, even of your esteem, and this because I ceased to believe that you still loved me after what had taken place! No," I went on, checking him again as he was about to interrupt me, "for once I must speak out all that has been torturing me so long! Was I to blame because I did not know life, and because you left me to find it out for myself?... And am I to blame that now,—when at last I comprehend, of myself, what is necessary in life; now, when for more than a year I have been making a struggle to return to you,—you constantly repulse me, constantly pretend not to know what I want? and things are so arranged that there is never anything for you to reproach yourself with, while I am left to be miserable and guilty? Yes, you would cast me back again into that life which must make wretchedness for me and for you!"

"And how am I doing that?" he asked, with sincere surprise and alarm.

"Did not you tell me yesterday,—yes, you tell me so perpetually,—that the life here does not suit me, and that we must go to St. Petersburg again for the winter? Instead of supporting me," I continued, "you avoid all frankness with me, any talk that is sweet, and real. And then if I fall, you will reproach me with it, or you will make light of it!"

"Stop, stop," he said severely and coldly; "what you are saying is not right. It only shows that you are badly disposed towards me, that you do not...."

"That I do not love you! say it! say it, then!" I exclaimed, blind with my tears. I sat down on the bench, and covered my face with my handkerchief.

"That is the way he understands me!" I thought, trying to control my choking sobs. "It is all over with our old love!" said the voice in my heart. He did not come near me, and made no attempt to console me. He was wounded by what I had said. His voice was calm and dry, as he began:

"I do not know what you have to reproach me with, except that I do not love you as I used to do!"

"As you used to love me!..." I murmured under my handkerchief, drenching it with bitter tears.

"And for that, time and ourselves are equally guilty. For each period there is one suitable phase of love...."

He was silent.

"And shall I tell you the whole truth, since you desire frankness? Just as, during that first year of our acquaintance, I spent night after night without sleep, thinking of you and building up my own love, until it grew to fill all my heart, so in St. Petersburg and while we were abroad I spent fearful nights in striving to break down and destroy this love which was my torment. I could not destroy it, but I did at least destroy the element which had tormented me; I became tranquil, and yet I continued to love you,—but it was with another love."

"And you call *that* love, when it was nothing but a punishment!" I replied. "Why did you let me live in the world, if it appeared to you so pernicious that because of it you would cease to love me?"

"It was not the world, my dear, that was the guilty one."

"Why did you not use your power? Why did you not strangle me? Murder me? That would have been better for me to-day than to have lost all that made my happiness,—it would have been better for me, and at least there would not have been the shame!"

I began to sob again, and I covered my face.

Just at that moment Macha and Sonia, wet and merry, ran up on the terrace, laughing and talking; but at the sight of us their voices were hushed, and they hurried into the house.

We remained where we were, for a long time, silent; after they were gone, I sobbed on until my tears were exhausted and I felt somewhat calmer. I looked at him. He was sitting with his head resting on his hand, and appeared to wish to say something to me in response to my glance, but he only gave a heavy sigh and put his head down again.

I went to him and drew his hand away. He turned then, and looked at me thoughtfully.

"Yes," he said, as if pursuing his own thoughts, "for all of us, and particularly for you women, it is necessary that we should ourselves lift to our own lips the cup of the vanities of life, before we can taste life itself; no one believes the experience of others. You had not, at that time, dipped very deep into the science of those entrancing and seducing vanities. Therefore I allowed you to plunge for a moment; I had no right to forbid it, simply because my own hour for it was long since over."

"Why did you let me live among these vanities, if you loved me?"

"Because you would not—nay, more, you could not—have believed me about them; it was necessary for you to learn for yourself; and you have learned."

"You reasoned a great deal," said I. "That was because you loved me so little."

We were silent again.

"What you have just said to me is hard, but it is the truth," he resumed, after a while, rising abruptly, and beginning to walk about the terrace; "yes, it is the truth! I have been to blame," he went on, stopping before me.... "Either I ought not to have let myself love you at all, or I ought to have loved you more simply—yes!"

"Sergius, let us forget everything," said I, timidly.

"No, what is gone never comes again, there can be no turning back ..." his voice softened as he spoke.

"It has already come again," said I, laying my hand on his shoulder.

He took the hand in his, and pressed it.

"No, I was not telling the truth, when I pretended not to regret the past; no, I do regret your past love; I bitterly mourn over it,—this love, which can no longer exist. Who is to blame? I do not know. Love there may even yet be, but not the same; its place is still there, but darkened and desolated; it is without savor and without strength; the remembrance has not vanished, nor the gratitude, but...."

"Do not speak so," I interrupted. "Let it come to life again, let it be what it was.... Might that be?" I asked, looking into his face. His eyes were serene, quiet, and met mine without their old deep look.

Even as I asked the question I felt the answer, felt that my wish was no longer possible to realize. He smiled; it seemed to me an old man's smile, gentle and full of peace.

"How young you still are, and how old I am already!" he said. "Why delude ourselves?" he added, still with the same smile.

I remained near him, silent, and feeling my soul grow more and more tranquil.

"Do not let us try to repeat life," he went on, "nor to lie to ourselves. But it is something, to have no longer, God willing, either disquiet or distress. We have nothing to seek for. We have already found, already shared, happiness enough. All we have to do now is to open the way,—you see to whom...." he said, pointing out little Vania, in his nurse's arms, at the terrace door. "That is necessary, dear love," he concluded, bending over me and dropping a kiss on my hair.

It was no longer a lover, it was an old friend who gave the caress.

The perfumed freshness of night was rising, sweeter and stronger, from the garden; the few sounds audible were solemn and far off, and soon gave way to deep tranquillity; one by one the stars shone out. I looked at him, and all at once I became conscious of infinite relief in my soul; it was as if a moral nerve, whose sensitiveness had caused me keen suffering had suddenly been removed. Quietly and clearly I comprehended that the dominant sentiment of this phase of my existence was irrevocably gone, as was the phase itself, and that not only was its return impossible, but that it would be to me full of unendurable pain. There had been enough of this time; and had it indeed been so good,—this time, which to me had seemed to enclose such joys? And already it had lasted so long, so long!

"But tea is waiting," he said, gently; and we went together to the drawing-room.

At the door I met Macha, and the nurse with Vania. I took the child in my arms, wrapped up the little bare feet, and, holding it close to my heart, barely touched its lips with a light kiss. Almost asleep as it was, it moved its little arms, stretched out the crumpled fingers, and opened its bewildered eyes, as if trying to find or remember something; all at once its eyes fell on me, a look of intelligence sparkled in them, and the pink pursed-up lips lengthened in a baby smile. "You are mine, mine!" thought I, with a delicious thrill running through me, and as I strained it to my heart I was half afraid of hurting it with my eager embrace. Over and over I kissed its cold little feet, its breast, its arms, and head with the scant covering of down. My husband came up to us, quickly drew the wrapping over the baby's face, then, drawing it away again:

"Ivan Sergevitch!" he said with finger under the little chin.

But I, in my turn, covered up Ivan Sergevitch. No one should look at him so long, except myself. I glanced at my husband, his eyes laughed as they rested on mine, and it was long since I had met his with such happy joy.

This day ended my romance with my husband. The old love remained, and the dear remembrance of what could never come back to me; but a new love for my children and my children's father, began another life and another way of happiness, up to this hour unending ... for at last I know that in home, and in the pure joys of home will be found—real happiness!

THE END

www.ingramcontent.com/pod-product-compliance
Ingram Content Group UK Ltd.
Pitfield, Milton Keynes, MK11 3LW, UK
UKHW040318300826
14791UKWH00003B/965

9 789354 629228